THE HOME BARTENDER

VODKA

CIDER MILL
PRESS

BOOK
PUBLISHERS

120+ ESSENTIAL COCKTAILS
for the **VODKA LOVER**

THE HOME BARTENDER: VODKA

13-Digit ISBN: 978-1-40034-619-6
10-Digit ISBN: 1-40034-619-3

This book may be ordered by mail from the publisher. Please include $5.99 for postage and handling. Please support your local bookseller first!

Books published by Cider Mill Press Book Publishers are available at special discounts for bulk purchases in the United States by corporations, institutions, and other organizations. For more information, please contact the publisher.

Cider Mill Press Book Publishers

"Where good books are ready for press"

501 Nelson Place
Nashville, Tennessee 37214
cidermillpress.com

Image Credits: Photos on pages 31, 32, 36, 43, 47, 78, 103, 120, 154, 162, 174, 188, 192, 199, 200, 211, 214, 235, 240, 243, 244, 252, 260, and 263 courtesy of Cider Mill Press.

All other images used under official license from Shutterstock.com.

Glassware icons by Shutterstock; all ingredient icons by Shutterstock or Cider Mill Press Book Publishers.

Printed in Malaysia

24 25 26 27 28 OFF 5 4 3 2 1
First Edition

CONTENTS

INTRODUCTION 5   SIMPLE SYRUP 7

TRIED AND TRUE 9

Long Island Express 10
Vodka Soda 13
Vodka Negroni 14
Classic Cosmopolitan 17
Perfect Comsopolitan 18
Budget Cosmopolitan 21
Cherry Lime Spike 22

Cherry Bomb 25
Greyhound 26
Screwdriver 29
Mason Jar Screwdriver 30
Harvey Wallbanger 33
Capescrew 34
Moscow Mule 37

Mint Mule 38
The Essential Bloody Mary 41
The Incredible Apicius
Bloody Mary 42
The Original Bloody Mary 45
Mason Jar Bloody Mary 46
The Dirty Spy 49

FRUITY REFRESHMENT 51

Sea Breeze 52
Ocean Breeze 55
Borrowed Thyme 56
By the Horns 59
Betty's Cosmo 60
Peach Tree Iced Tea 63
Ginger Binger 64

Sage Advice 67
Sex on the Beach 68
Melon Ball 71
Lycheetini 72
Hairy Navel 75
Melon Refresher 76
Grape Chill 79

Early Riser 80
The Slammer 83
100% Winter Vitamin 84
Sunny Day 87
Herbal Affirmation 88

CANDY-COATED NOSTALGIA 91

Creamsicle 93
Strawberries and Cream 94
Pear Pressure 97
Quickslide 98
Godmother 101
Blastoff 102
Cherry Swizzle 105
Cherry Tootsie Pop 106

Chocolate Cream
and Peaches 109
Gumball 110
Head Rush 113
Jolly Rancher 114
Pink Petals 117
Poison Apple 118
Purple Hooter 121
Storm Warning 122

Woo Hoo 125
Absolut Bitch 126
Teddy Bear 129
Vanilla Pear 130
Rose Salt Dog 133
Ruby Twilite 134
Rose de Varsovie 137

PARTY FAVORS 139

Wedded Bliss 140
Ring #4 143
Ring #5 144
Summer Splash 147
Liquid Apple Pie 148
Vodka Sunrise 151

Drink the C 152
Butterbrew 155
Cape Cod 156
Gingerbread 159
Angel's Kiss 160
Hell's Gate 163

Choco Peat 164
Bona Dea 167
Jungle Punch 168
Bisous du Soleil 171
Mr. Funk 172
Amelia 175

SWEET AND SOURS 177

Blue Fireflies 178
Vodka Gimlet 181
Kamikaze 182
A Little Lem 185
Appletini 186
Blue Lagoon 189

Citrus Sunset 190
Grape Sourball 193
Great Idea 194
Chilton 197
Vineyard Splash 198
Berries from the West 201

Raspberry Twist 202
Pink Panther 205
Pink Lemonade 206
Lemonade Shocker 209
Lemon Drop 210

COFFEE CONCOCTIONS 213

White Russian 215
Classic White Russian 216
Fancy White Russian 219

Mocha Mocha Mocha 220
Mind Eraser 223
Espresso Martini 224

Deep Throat 227
Dangerous Grandma 228
Mason Jar Mudslide 231

MAGNIFICENT MARTINIS 233

Classic Vodka Martini 234
Budget Vodka Martini 237
Purist's Vodka Martini 238
Dry Vodka Martini 241
Wet Vodka Martini 242
Perfect Vodka Martini 245

Dirty Vodka Martini 246
Bellini Martini 249
Birthday Martini 250
Raspberry Martini 253
Sour Cherry Martini 254
French Martini de Nancy 257

Vesper Martini 258
Spicy Martini 261
McClure's Pickle Martini 262
Pickled Martini 265

INDEX 266

INTRODUCTION

Cocktails can be complicated. With so many drinks featuring what feels like dozens of ingredients, being mixed together in increasingly complicated and diverse ways, it isn't hard to feel out of your depth when it comes to mixology.

But it doesn't have to be that way! Some of the best cocktails in the world feature only a couple of ingredients, shaken or stirred together in straightforward proportions, and ready to drink in seconds. Everyone knows that sometimes simplicity is the way to go—not just for the sake of convenience, but for taste as well. After all, who needs eight different ingredients muddling their flavors together, when all you really want is something to accent the great taste of your whiskey?

The Home Bartender series features the best of the best when it comes to simple cocktails. With classic cocktails you'll recognize and new drinks you're sure to love, there's something for everyone here. Whether you're looking for some novel and unique drinks or to bust out an old and timeless recipe, *The Home Bartender: Vodka* is the perfect book for any home bar!

BAR TOOLS

Sometimes mixing a drink is as simple as pouring the ingredients. Other times, you need to do a little more. Bar tools are there to make your life a bit easier when it comes to mixing up these more complicated cocktails. From the cocktail shaker to the muddler, these are the tools that you would be wise to have in your home bar.

Must-Haves

Cocktail Shaker
Strainer
Jigger
Knife
Bottle Opener
Corkscrew

Nice to Have

Cocktail Stirrer
Muddler
Juicer
Zester

GLASSWARE

Must-Haves	Nice to Have	Wish List
Pint Glass	Margarita Glass	Hurricane Glass
Shot Glass	Cocktail Glass	Daiquiri Glass
Rocks Glass	Champagne Flute	Irish Coffee Glass
Highball Glass	Mason Jar	Sour Glass

The Russian love of vodka is undisputed. The same can't be said, however, for the country that can rightfully claim to have invented the potent spirit. There are historical records that allude to vodka being produced in Poland as early as the eighth century and in Russia in the ninth century. Records that explicitly name vodka—which incidentally derives from the Slavic word for "water," voda—exist in Poland's Sandomierz Court Registry dating back to 1405, while any existing written records of vodka in Russia don't appear until 1751.

While potatoes are commonly a primary ingredient in vodka, the tubers didn't even show up in Europe until the sixteenth century, when the Spanish Conquistadors returned from South America with them. So the earliest vodkas were sugar- and grain-based. Vodka can also be made from grapes and whey, as well as carrots, beets, and several other ingredients; today, most commercial vodkas are made with fermented grains, like rice, wheat, rye, or sorghum.

Whatever the base starch being used, water and enzymes are added to it in order to convert the starch to sugar, before adding yeast to begin the fermentation process. In the early days of vodka production, wild airborne yeast was part of the equation (which was really more like magic—hence the associations with alchemy), but today it is all automated and regulated. The distillation process then begins, vaporizing the low ABV liquid as it moves through column stills and extracting impurities until the end result is a very high-percentage alcohol, which is then diluted and flavored before bottling. Vodka is best stored in the freezer. With a minimum 40 percent ABV, the drink has a lot of "heat" to it, and when kept cold, the heat is tempered, allowing the body and depth of the vodka to be appreciated, whether one is doing shots or mixing cocktails.

The location of the distillery and what the distillers have the easiest access to will generally govern what is used to create vodka. Many countries use grain to make their vodka, with potatoes being a close second. Each has different advantages, since potatoes have a high level of starch that imparts a creamy, oily mouthfeel and a natural, light sweetness, while grains are thought to produce a cleaner spirit that is easier to pair with other ingredients.

Vodka is the tofu of spirits. This comparison is a compliment. Some people love drinking vodka straight; they love vodka's lack of a strong taste and its relatively low calorie count, and it is their spirit of choice for doing shots. But vodka's lack of a strong flavor profile makes it a perfect spirit for cocktails. It plays well with many other spirits and complements whatever it is added to, which is not something you can say about all other types of alcohol.

If there's one kind of liquor that people tend to have lying around the house, it's vodka. And for good reason! Sometimes the very best cocktails are those thrown together with whatever you happened to have nearby. In many ways, vodka embodies the true spirit (pun intended) of the Home Bartender series. In the following pages, you'll find recipes both old and new, familiar and unfamiliar, with a new spin on some classic tastes and a variety of different ways to inject a little boozy goodness into a simple mix of flavors.

SIMPLE SYRUP

Place 1 cup of sugar and 1 cup of water in a saucepan and bring to a boil, stirring to dissolve the sugar. Remove the pan from heat and let the syrup cool completely before using or storing.

TRIED AND TRUE

You can never go wrong with a classic—that's what makes it so iconic. It's timeless, appealing to just about everybody, and hard to mess up. These vodka cocktails are sweet simplicity itself: some have only two ingredients. Like with the Greyhound or the Screwdriver, sometimes all you need is vodka and juice. We've even included a simplified Bloody Mary (see page 41), though don't fear if you're someone who likes all the bells and whistles—you'll find those versions in this chapter too!

LONG ISLAND EXPRESS

The Long Island Iced Tea is one of the most popular (and strong) cocktails on planet Earth, but it has far more than the five ingredients found here (in fact, it has more than five different liquors alone). Still, the spirit of the cocktail should live on, and it does just that in the Long Island Express. Trimming some of the fat (not literal fat—that would be disgusting) from the original recipe, we are left with a simple vodka-and-cola, with a few extra ingredients to ensure that you won't want for flavor.

INGREDIENTS

 ½ lemon (juiced)

 1 oz. vodka

 2 oz. Coca-Cola

 1 splash of triple sec

 1 lemon wheel (garnish)

GLASSWARE
 Highball glass

1 Juice the lemon over ice, then add the vodka and splash of triple sec to your highball glass.

2 Add the cola to fill, then stir until thoroughly mixed.

3 Garnish with the lemon wheel.

VODKA SODA

Nostalgia is en vogue right now, and it's not difficult to see why. Looking back on the past can spur powerful emotions. For many of us, early adulthood was a time for new experiences—and who could forget their first time in a bar? Of course, when you're barely 21, you order what you know—and a classic Vodka Soda always brings back memories of those days gone by.

INGREDIENTS

 1 oz. vodka

 1 splash of lime juice

 3 oz. club soda

 1 lime wheel (garnish)

GLASSWARE

 Highball glass or mason jar

1   Add the vodka and lime juice to a highball glass or mason jar and stir together. Add ice.

2   Add the club soda to fill.

3   Garnish with the lime wheel.

VODKA NEGRONI

True, the Negroni is typically made with gin, but if all you've got is vodka, you can adapt it fairly easily. You can add a splash of crème de menthe to replace the notes of juniper provided by the gin and give the drink a little minty freshness. Just don't add too much, or it'll overwhelm the flavor of the drink. But all in all, this is a clever little spin on a classic cocktail.

INGREDIENTS

 1 oz. vodka

 1 oz. Campari

 1 oz. sweet vermouth

 1 splash of crème de menthe

 1 orange slice (garnish)

GLASSWARE
 Rocks glass

1 Fill a mixing glass with ice and add the vodka, Campari, and sweet vermouth. Stir until thoroughly mixed.

2 Strain the resulting mixture into a rocks glass filled with ice.

3 Top with the splash of crème de menthe and garnish with the orange slice.

CLASSIC COSMOPOLITAN

Known for being fruity, delicious, and, well, pink, the Cosmopolitan is one of the tastiest and most popular vodka drinks around. Oddly, men tend to shy away from ordering the Cosmopolitan. It's a shame, really. It's the same color as a Cape Cod or a Greyhound, and it's served in more or less the same way as a Martini. Regardless, the Cosmopolitan is a delicious drink, perfect for a night out on the town or a cozy night in the apartment.

INGREDIENTS

 2 oz. Skyy Vodka

 1 oz. triple sec

 1 oz. cranberry juice

 1 splash of lime juice

 1 lime wedge (garnish)

GLASSWARE
 Cocktail glass

1 Fill a cocktail shaker with ice and add the liquid ingredients. Shake well.

2 Strain the resulting mixture into a cocktail glass and garnish with the lime wedge.

PERFECT COSMOPOLITAN

If you're drinking a classic cocktail like the Cosmopolitan, why not go all the way with it? Use only the finest ingredients, and you might be surprised to discover that this already-delicious treat can actually get even tastier. Make sure you're using the freshest ingredients too—that means fresh-squeezed limes only!

INGREDIENTS

 2 oz. Grey Goose Vodka

 1 oz. triple sec

 1 oz. cranberry juice

 1 lime wedge (juiced)

 1 lime wheel (garnish)

 GLASSWARE
Cocktail glass

1 Fill a cocktail shaker with ice and add the vodka, triple sec, cranberry juice, and lime juice (squeeze the lime straight in). Shake well.

2 Strain the resulting mixture into a cocktail glass and garnish with the lime wheel.

BUDGET COSMOPOLITAN

Then again, why go over-the-top for a cocktail that's really little more than a mixture of three different fruit flavors, with a splash of vodka thrown in for good measure? If that's your mentality, then maybe the Budget Cosmo is for you. Never mind the garnishes, and who needs fresh limes? Grab the vodka you've got on the shelf, mix it up until it's nice and pink, and presto! Deliciousness.

INGREDIENTS

 2 oz. Svedka Vodka

 1 oz. triple sec

 1 oz. cranberry juice

 1 splash of lime juice

GLASSWARE
 Cocktail glass

1 Fill a cocktail shaker with ice and add the vodka, triple sec, cranberry juice, and lime juice. Shake well.

2 Strain the resulting mixture into a cocktail glass.

CHERRY LIME SPIKE

Cherry and lime have traditionally gone well together, but rather than drink a regular old glass of cherry limeade, why not spike it with vodka? A little cherry vodka can go a long way, both in terms of adding alcohol to the cocktail and adding flavor.

INGREDIENTS

 1 oz. cherry vodka

 1 oz. lime juice

 2 oz. club soda

 1 dash of grenadine

 1 lime wheel (garnish)

GLASSWARE

 Highball glass

1 Pour the cherry vodka and lime juice into a highball glass and stir together. Add ice.

2 Add the club soda to fill, then top with the small dash of grenadine for color.

3 Garnish with the lime wheel.

CHERRY BOMB

If you love the sweet taste of cherries, you will surely love the Cherry Bomb! This twist on a Vodka Red Bull will become your go-to shot.

INGREDIENTS

 1 maraschino cherry

 1 oz. cherry vodka

 1 oz. Red Bull

GLASSWARE

 Shot glass

1　Place maraschino cherries in each shot glass.

2　Add the cherry vodka and Red Bull to a cocktail shaker filled with ice. Shake vigorously for 15 to 20 seconds, and strain into the shot glass.

GREYHOUND

If you are looking for a tart and refreshing drink, look no further! The addition of grapefruit juice introduces an energizing touch to this drink, though canned or bottled grapefruit juice is also a great choice.

INGREDIENTS

 I oz. vodka

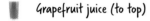 Grapefruit juice (to top)

GLASSWARE
Highball glass

1 Build in a highball glass filled with ice.

SCREWDRIVER

This drink was created by American oil workers in the Persian Gulf who were looking to add an extra kick to their orange juice. The iconic Screwdriver was given its name for the tool used to mix the drink when there weren't any spoons at the ready. This classic is a refreshing base for many other cocktails.

INGREDIENTS

 1 oz. vodka

 Orange juice (to top)

1 orange slice (garnish)

GLASSWARE

Highball glass

1 Build in a highball glass filled with ice.

2 Garnish with the orange slice.

MASON JAR SCREWDRIVER

A spin on the classic Screwdriver, this rendition is perfect for front-porch sipping. The addition of pomegranate juice for the rim and an orange wheel for garnish dresses this drink up, making it ideal for casual get-togethers!

INGREDIENTS

 I oz. vodka

 2 oz. orange juice (to top)

 I dash of pomegranate juice (for the rim)

 I orange wheel (garnish)

GLASSWARE

 Mason jar

1 Fill a mason jar with ice, add the vodka, and top with the orange juice.

2 Dab a finger into the pomegranate juice and rub it along the rim of the jar.

3 Garnish with the orange wheel.

HARVEY WALLBANGER

Tom Harvey is to thank for this spin on the Screwdriver, after notoriously ordering an addition of Galliano to his drink after long days of surfing in Manhattan Beach, California. The sweet and tangy flavor from the fresh orange juice pairs deliciously with the herbal undertones of the Galliano.

INGREDIENTS

 1 oz. vodka

 4 oz. fresh orange juice

 ¼ oz. Galliano (to top)

 1 orange slice (garnish)

GLASSWARE

 Collins glass

1 Pour the vodka and fresh orange juice into an ice-filled Collins glass.

2 Float the Galliano on top and garnish with the orange slice.

CAPESCREW

Two of the most famous vodka cocktails are the Screwdriver, traditionally consisting of vodka and orange juice, and the Cape Cod, made with vodka and cranberry juice. Well, as any seasoned breakfaster will surely tell you, few flavors go together quite as well as orange juice and cranberry juice. Mixed together, they create a flavor combination of sweet and tart that can tantalize any palate. Add in a little vodka and triple sec, and you've got the Capescrew, a combination of two favorites that takes both to the next level.

INGREDIENTS

 1 oz. vodka

 1 splash of triple sec

 1 oz. orange juice

 1 oz. cranberry juice

 1 orange wheel (garnish)

GLASSWARE

 Highball glass

1 Pour the vodka over ice in a highball glass and add the splash of triple sec.

2 Add the orange juice and cranberry juice and stir until thoroughly mixed.

3 Garnish with the orange wheel.

MOSCOW MULE

Cocktail lore is full of cock-and-bull stories, but the history of the Moscow Mule is well-documented and can be pinpointed to a day in 1941 when three lives converged at the Cock'n Bull pub on the Sunset Strip in Los Angeles. John Martin, the recently minted owner of the financially struggling Smirnoff Vodka distillery, was commiserating with his friend Jack Morgan, owner of the Cock'n Bull, who at the time was trying to launch his own brand of ginger beer. Enter Sophie Berezinski: the Russian immigrant had arrived in America with 2,000 copper mugs that she had designed and her father had stamped out on his press. One day she happened into Morgan's bar, to find two men lamenting their entrepreneurial woes. Together Berezinski, Martin, and Morgan would develop a cocktail that married ginger beer, vodka, and the cooling properties of copper to make the Moscow Mule.

INGREDIENTS

 Juice of ½ lime

 1 oz. vodka

 3 oz. ginger beer (to top)

 1 lime wheel (garnish)

 1 sprig of mint (garnish)

GLASSWARE

 Copper mug

1 Place the lime juice in a copper mug and add the desired amount of ice. Add the vodka and top with the ginger beer.

2 Garnish with the lime wheel and sprig of mint.

MINT MULE

The Moscow Mule is a popular vodka cocktail featuring primarily vodka and ginger beer. The sharpness of each of those flavors makes this a winning combination, but sometimes it can be a bit much. The Moscow Mule is typically tempered with a bit of lime juice, but let's further take it down by adding a bit of mint to the party as well.

INGREDIENTS

 6 mint leaves

 1 lime wedge (juiced)

 1 oz. vodka

 2 oz. ginger beer

 1 lime wheel (garnish)

GLASSWARE

 Copper mug or highball glass

1 Tear the mint leaves in half to release the flavor, then add them to the bottom of a highball glass or copper mug.

2 Add the juice from the lime wedge and muddle the mint leaves. Add ice.

3 Pour in the vodka and ginger beer. Stir until thoroughly mixed.

4 Garnish with the lime wheel.

THE ESSENTIAL BLOODY MARY

The Essential Bloody Mary takes the Bloody Mary and distills (no pun intended) it down to its most fundamental ingredients for your mixing pleasure.

INGREDIENTS

 I dash of Worcestershire sauce

 I dash of lemon juice

 I oz. vodka

 2 oz. tomato juice

Garnish with anything your heart desires

 GLASSWARE
Rocks glass

1 Add the Worcestershire sauce and lemon juice to a rocks glass, then add ice.

2 Pour in the vodka and tomato juice and stir until thoroughly mixed.

3 Garnish with bacon, olives, lime wedges, celery, pickles, an entire hamburger, or anything else your heart desires.

THE INCREDIBLE APICIUS BLOODY MARY

Perfect for Bloody Mary fans looking for a little more of a kick, The Incredible Apicius Bloody Mary is packed with delicious flavors. The blend of spicy and sweet in this drink makes it a must try!

INGREDIENTS

 1 cup cherry tomatoes

 4 drops of Tabasco Chipotle

 2 dashes of white balsamic reduction

 1¾ oz. cranberry juice

 ¾ oz. vodka

 1 dash of black pepper

 3 drops of The Bitter End Memphis Barbecue Bitters

 3 pinches of celery salt

GLASSWARE
Cocktail glass

1. Place the cherry tomatoes in a cocktail shaker and crush them.

2. Add the Tabasco Chipotle, balsamic reduction, cranberry juice, vodka, pepper, bitters, and celery salt. Shake vigorously for 20 seconds.

3. Double strain into a chilled cocktail glass.

THE ORIGINAL BLOODY MARY

Synonymous with the hair-of-the-dog hangover cure, and ubiquitous as the beverage of choice for a brunch bender, the Bloody Mary is known by one and all, even those who don't like its tangy bite. Like with most classic cocktails, there is no certain origin story for the Bloody Mary, but Russians (and their vodka) fleeing the Revolution, starting around 1920, and the growing popularity of American canned tomato juice, certainly serve as the seeds for the drink. We might never know exactly who came up with the drink, though most agree that famed bartender Fernand Petiot popularized early iterations of it, first at Harry's New York Bar in Paris, and then at the King Cole Bar at the St. Regis Hotel in Manhattan, where he served up something called the "Red Snapper," which included the spices and seasonings associated with the drink today.

INGREDIENTS

 4 dashes of salt

 2 dashes of cayenne pepper

 2 dashes of ground black pepper

 6 dashes of Worcestershire sauce

 2 dashes of lemon juice

 2 oz. vodka

 2 oz. tomato juice

GLASSWARE

Collins glass

1 Place the salt, cayenne, and black pepper (be sure to use ground pepper instead of cracked pepper) in a Collins glass.

2 Fill with ice and then add the Worcestershire sauce, lemon juice, vodka, and tomato juice. Stir until combined.

MASON JAR BLOODY MARY

The classic Bloody Mary finds new life in this easy-sipping variation. With ingredients you would never have thought to put in a cocktail, this drink amazes with its ability to harness chaos into a symphony of flavors.

INGREDIENTS

 Juice of 1 lime wedge

 Old Bay Seasoning (for the rim)

 2 oz. vodka

 ½ oz. olive brine

 2 dashes of horseradish

 Tomato juice (to top)

 3 drops of Worcestershire sauce

 3 dashes of hot sauce

 2 dashes of pepper

 2 dashes of celery salt

 1 celery stalk, 3 olives, or cooked bacon (garnish)

GLASSWARE

Mason jar

1 Wet the rim of a mason jar with the lime wedge and then dip the glass into Old Bay Seasoning.

2 Add ice and the vodka, olive brine, lime juice, and horseradish, and then top with tomato juice. Leave enough space to stir. Stir until thoroughly combined.

3 Add the Worcestershire sauce, hot sauce, pepper, and celery salt. Stir again until combined.

4 Garnish with either the celery stalk, olives, or rasher of bacon.

THE DIRTY SPY

The Vodka Martini is, of course, the drink that James Bond made famous, though it was already one of the most popular drinks in the world when 007 put in his first order. Martini drinkers will know that the iconic spy's request for his cocktail to be "shaken, not stirred" was an unusual one, as the Martini is not typically prepared this way. In honor of this unusual ask, The Dirty Spy is a simple Dirty Martini prepared in a cocktail shaker.

INGREDIENTS

3 oz. vodka

1 oz. dry vermouth

1 splash of green olive brine

1 pimento-stuffed green olive
(or more, for garnish)

GLASSWARE

Cocktail glass

1 Add the vodka, vermouth, and olive brine to a cocktail shaker filled with ice. Shake well.

2 Strain the resulting mixture into a cocktail glass and garnish with the olive (or a few).

FRUITY REFRESHMENT

Vodka is well-known for being a light spirit that pairs easily with anything. This makes it the ideal base for a refreshing cocktail in the summer heat or at the end of a long day. Take that and combine it with the rejuvenating power of fruit, and you've got a whole chapter full of drinks ready to cool you down and replenish your spirit. From the Sea Breeze to the Sex on the Beach, these cocktails will make you feel like you're on vacation.

SEA BREEZE

A traditional vodka cocktail, the Sea Breeze plays with a variety of citrus flavors to create a sweet concoction, perfect for relaxing on the beach on a hot summer day. Grapefruit, cranberry, and lime juice bounce off one another as the drink reaches your tongue, providing a cool, crisp, and refreshing counterbalance to the sun beating down on you.

INGREDIENTS

 ½ lime (juiced)

 1 oz. vodka

 1 oz. cranberry juice

 1 oz. grapefruit juice

 1 lime wedge (garnish)

 1 cherry (garnish)

GLASSWARE

 Highball glass

1   Juice the lime half over ice in a highball glass, then add the vodka.

2   Add the cranberry juice and grapefruit juice and stir until thoroughly mixed.

3   Garnish with the lime wedge and cherry.

OCEAN BREEZE

Looking for a tasty recipe that will serve your next big get-together? The deliciously citrusy Ocean Breeze is certain to please.

INGREDIENTS

 1 oz. vodka

 1 oz. gin

 1 oz. grapefruit juice

 3 oz. cranberry juice

 1 oz. Sprite (to top)

 1 lime wheel (garnish)

 1 cherry (garnish)

GLASSWARE
 Highball glass

1 Combine all of the liquid ingredients, except for the Sprite, in a highball glass filled with ice. Stir until thoroughly mixed.

2 Top with the Sprite and garnish with the lime wheel and cherry.

BORROWED THYME

Borrowed Thyme is similar to the Blastoff cocktail (see page 102), but it abandons the lemon and lime elements in favor of more herbal notes. If you've ever had thyme-infused lemonade, you know that it's an herb that works very well with citrus. Borrowed Thyme capitalizes on that, mixing thyme and grapefruit to create a taste that is sure to delight.

INGREDIENTS

 1 oz. vodka

 1 oz. club soda

 3 oz. grapefruit juice

 4 sprigs of thyme

GLASSWARE

 Rocks glass

1. Add the vodka, club soda, and grapefruit juice and 3 sprigs of the thyme to a rocks glass filled with ice.

2. Stir until thoroughly mixed.

3. Strain the resulting mixture into a rocks glass filled with ice.

4. Garnish with the remaining sprig of thyme.

BY THE HORNS

Maybe you're getting ready for a night on the town. Maybe you're heading out to see a show or a sporting event. Nothing gets your blood pumping and excitement brewing like a quick and dirty pregame drink. And if you want to get amped up, why not give yourself a boost of energy while you're at it? This drink calls for Red Bull, but really, you can use your energy drink of choice. The goal here is to balance the harsh buzz of the energy drink with the refreshing sweetness of grapefruit and lime, resulting in something easy to drink that will give you the jolt you need on your way out the door.

INGREDIENTS

 1 oz. vodka

 1 oz. grapefruit juice

 1 splash of lime juice

 1 oz. Red Bull (to top)

 1 lime wedge (garnish)

GLASSWARE

Rocks glass

1   Add the vodka, grapefruit juice, and lime juice to a cocktail shaker filled with ice. Shake well.

2   Strain the resulting mixture into a rocks glass filled with ice and top with the Red Bull.

3   Add the lime wedge for garnish.

BETTY'S COSMO

If you love Cosmos and want to try something a little bit different, give Betty's Cosmo a try. With equal parts vodka and cranberry juice cocktail, and a tantalizing mixture of fresh lime juice and its sweetened counterparts, Betty's Cosmo is a delicious drink, perfect for serving at family gatherings or sipping on the back porch.

INGREDIENTS

 3 oz. Skyy Vodka

 3 oz. cranberry juice cocktail

 1 oz. Cointreau

 1 dash of Rose's Sweetened Lime Juice

 1 squeeze of fresh lime juice

GLASSWARE

 Cocktail glass

1 Add the vodka, cranberry juice cocktail, Cointreau, and Rose's Sweetened Lime Juice to a cocktail shaker filled with ice. Shake well.

2 Strain the resulting mixture into a cocktail glass.

3 Top with the squeeze of fresh lime juice.

PEACH TREE ICED TEA

What's better than a little peach iced tea on a summer day? Iced tea is one of the most refreshing drinks on the planet, so adding a little vodka to the mix can't go awry. And where better to get that peach flavor that makes you feel all warm and fuzzy than by adding a little peach schnapps? Peach Tree Iced Tea is a drink that towers over other iced tea cocktails. Is it the best one out there? You be the judge.

INGREDIENTS

 6 mint leaves

 1 oz. peach schnapps

 1 oz. vodka

 2 oz. iced tea

GLASSWARE

 Highball glass

1. Tear the mint leaves in half and add them to the bottom of a highball glass. Add the peach schnapps and muddle together.

2. Add ice to the glass, and then pour in the vodka and iced tea. Stir until thoroughly mixed.

GINGER BINGER

Ginger goes well with vodka, and while ginger beer is always a popular cocktail ingredient, ginger ale has none of the harsh bite that ginger beer all too often imparts to cocktails. Ginger ale, a subtle background upon which to build, allows other flavors to come forward and contribute to the cocktail's flavor profile, as the orange and grapefruit do here.

INGREDIENTS

 1 oz. vodka

 1 splash of triple sec

 1 oz. grapefruit juice

 2 oz. ginger ale (to top)

 1 lime wheel (garnish)

 1 sprig of mint (garnish)

GLASSWARE

 Highball glass

1   Fill a highball glass with ice and add the vodka, triple sec, and grapefruit juice. Stir together.

2   Top with the ginger ale and stir again. Garnish with the lime wheel and sprig of mint.

SAGE ADVICE

Kombucha is having a moment. For those who aren't familiar with this bubbly fermented tea, it is extremely versatile, coming in a wide range of forms and flavors. Many of these flavors go extremely well with alcohol—especially strawberry/sage. If you can find this particular flavor of kombucha, give this delicious beverage a try. You'll find that the tartness of the kombucha plays nicely against the orange vodka, while sweet, smooth grenadine mellows everything out.

INGREDIENTS

 1 oz. orange vodka

 1 oz. strawberry/sage kombucha

 1 oz. strawberry seltzer

 1 splash of grenadine

 1 handful of sliced strawberries (garnish)

GLASSWARE

 Highball glass

1 Add the orange vodka, kombucha, and seltzer to a highball glass filled with ice.

2 Stir thoroughly.

3 Top with the grenadine and garnish with the sliced strawberries.

SEX ON THE BEACH

Looking for a perfect summer cocktail? The Sex on the Beach is a refreshing blend of citrusy and tart flavors—an excellent way to cool off during those hotter days!

INGREDIENTS

 ½ oz. vodka

 1 oz. peach schnapps

 2 oz. orange juice (to top)

 2 oz. cranberry juice (to top)

 1 orange slice (garnish)

 1 cherry (garnish)

GLASSWARE
 Collins glass

1 Add the vodka and peach schnapps to a Collins glass filled with ice.

2 Top with the orange juice and cranberry juice. Garnish with the orange slice and cherry.

MELON BALL

The Melon Ball is another classic, refreshing cocktail to add to your drink collection this summer. This drink is ideal for those seeking a sweet and subtly earthy flavor.

INGREDIENTS

 1 oz. vodka

 ½ oz. Midori (to top)

 orange juice (to top)

 1 dehydrated orange slice (garnish)

GLASSWARE
 Goblet or rocks glass

1 Pour the vodka into a goblet or rocks glass filled with ice. Top with orange juice.

2 Float the Midori on top and garnish with the dehydrated orange slice.

LYCHEETINI

If you are a fan of lychees, this is the drink for you! The Lycheetini is an inventive take on the Martini that introduces a hint of tropical flavor.

INGREDIENTS

 3 oz. vodka

 1 oz. triple sec

 2 oz. lychee liqueur

 1 lychee (garnish)

GLASSWARE
 Cocktail glass

1 Add the vodka, triple sec, and lychee liqueur to a cocktail shaker filled with ice and shake vigorously.

2 Strain the resulting mixture into a cocktail glass.

3 Garnish with the lychee, skewered on a toothpick.

HAIRY NAVEL

This is another refreshing drink to try during the hot weather. The mélange of fruit flavors in this drink makes it feel luxurious without requiring extra effort to put it together.

 1½ oz. vodka

 1½ oz. peach schnapps

 4 oz. orange juice (to top)

 1 splash of pineapple juice

 1 orange slice (garnish)

 1 sprig of mint (garnish)

GLASSWARE

 Mason jar

1. Fill a mason jar with the desired amount of ice, and then add the vodka and peach schnapps. Stir together.

2. Top with the orange juice and small splash of pineapple juice.

3. Garnish with the orange slice and mint sprig.

MELON REFRESHER

Another deliciously sweet drink for those who just can't get enough. The Melon Refresher provides exactly what its name promises for those warm-weather days: refreshment!

INGREDIENTS

 1 oz. melon liqueur

 1 oz. vodka

 4 oz. lemon-lime soda (to top)

 Lime wheels (garnish)

GLASSWARE

 Mason jar

1   Place the desired amount of ice in a mason jar, and then add the melon liqueur and vodka.

2   Top with the lemon-lime soda.

3   Garnish with a few lime wheels.

GRAPE CHILL

Who says wine gets all the alcoholic glory? The Grape Chill proves that grape works just as well in a vodka cocktail, and the vanilla and pineapple elevate the whole concoction to the next level.

INGREDIENTS

 2 oz. grape vodka

 1 oz. vanilla

 1 oz. pineapple juice

 Green grapes (garnish)

GLASSWARE
Shot glasses

1 Combine all of the ingredients, except for the garnish, in a cocktail shaker filled with ice. Shake vigorously for 15 to 20 seconds.

2 Strain into shot glasses.

3 Garnish each glass with a green grape skewered on a toothpick.

EARLY RISER

Looking for a new hangover cure? Look no further. Early mornings have never been so easy! The citrus of the orange juice pairs beautifully with the sweet vermouth, to make waking up a real treat.

INGREDIENTS

 1 oz. vodka

 3 oz. orange juice

 1 oz. sweet vermouth (to top)

 1 splash of club soda

 1 strip of orange peel (garnish)

 GLASSWARE
Cocktail glass

1 Combine the vodka and orange juice in a cocktail glass filled with ice and stir.

2 Top with the sweet vermouth and add the splash of club soda.

3 Garnish with the strip of orange peel.

THE SLAMMER

The combination of amaretto and Southern Comfort creates a sweet, nutty taste, which is complemented perfectly by the orange juice. This drink is served in a punch bowl without ice, so as not to water down the cocktail!

INGREDIENTS

 1 oz. vodka

 1 oz. amaretto

 1 oz. Southern Comfort

 3 oz. orange juice

 orange wheels (garnish)

GLASSWARE
 Punch bowl

1. Combine all of the ingredients, except for the garnish, in a large punch bowl. Stir until thoroughly mixed.

2. Garnish with orange wheels. Do not add ice (though ice should be made available).

100% WINTER VITAMIN

The 100% Winter Vitamin is so full of fruits and vegetables that it almost counts as a health drink! Maybe don't drive to the gym after this one, though.

INGREDIENTS

 1³/₄ oz. vodka

 2 teaspoons Cynar

 2 teaspoons Aperol

 2 teaspoons honey

 2 teaspoons lime

 2 spoonfuls of apricot/yuzu jam

 1³/₄ oz. fresh carrot-apple juice

 2 dashes of celery bitters

GLASSWARE
 Small carafe or bowl

1 Combine all of the ingredients in a cocktail shaker filled with ice. Shake vigorously.

2 Strain into a small carafe or bowl.

SUNNY DAY

It's become almost cliché to "drown your sorrows" in alcohol, but the truth is, it's never a good idea. Still, there are times when you need a little pick-me-up to boost your spirits, and you might be surprised how much a well-made cocktail can buoy your mood. The Sunny Day is the perfect cocktail for just such an occasion. Balancing sweet vermouth and bitter Campari against the floral notes of elderflower liqueur, the Sunny Day offers a delicate complexity sure to take your mind off whatever ails you.

INGREDIENTS

 I oz. vodka

 I oz. Campari

 I oz. elderflower liqueur

 I oz. sweet vermouth

 I lime wedge (juiced)

 I orange slice (garnish)

GLASSWARE

 Rocks glass

1 Add the vodka, Campari, elderflower liqueur, and sweet vermouth to a cocktail shaker filled with ice. Shake well.

2 Strain the resulting mixture into a rocks glass containing the desired amount of ice.

3 Squeeze the lime wedge into the glass. Garnish with the orange slice.

HERBAL AFFIRMATION

A date-night cocktail should be fun. Something light, refreshing, and whimsical. Building a cocktail around kombucha is a great way to go—there are so many flavors to choose from, and the fizzy, acidic nature of the drink really packs in a lot of flavor. Herbal kombuchas, in particular, bring a unique element to the table, and this lavender kombucha is no exception. Thanks to its light-purple coloration, a little bit of blue curaçao turns this cocktail a deep, rich shade of cobalt—one that's sure to impress your date.

INGREDIENTS

 2 oz. vodka

 1 oz. lemon juice

 1 oz. blue curaçao

 2 oz. lavender kombucha (to top)

GLASSWARE

 Rocks glass

1 Add the vodka, lemon juice, and blue curaçao to a cocktail shaker filled with ice. Shake well.

2 Strain the resulting mixture into a rocks glass filled with ice.

3 Top with the lavender kombucha.

CANDY-COATED NOSTALGIA

We all remember the excitement of enjoying sweet treats as children. Whether it was trick-or-treating on Halloween or just getting a lollipop at the doctor's office, a little dose of sugar could take a good day to a great one. Some things change as we grow up, but for most of us, these treats still spark something in us, and remind us of the simpler days of our youth. Have a Creamsicle, a Gumball, or a Jolly Rancher, and feel your childlike wonder come alive once more.

CREAMSICLE

If you're like us, you grew up eating Creamsicle Popsicles, and this drink captures that flavor. This delicious combination of orange and cream will sweep you straight back to your childhood on a wave of nostalgia— with an adult twist.

INGREDIENTS

 1 oz. vodka

 1 oz. orange juice

 1 oz. cream

 1 splash of triple sec

 1 orange slice (garnish)

GLASSWARE

 Rocks glass

1 Stir all of the ingredients, except for the garnish, together in a mixing glass.

2 Strain the resulting mixture into a rocks glass filled with ice.

3 Garnish with the orange slice.

STRAWBERRIES AND CREAM

The Creamsicle is a delicious drink, but the orange isn't the only fruit known to pair well with cream. Enter the Strawberries and Cream cocktail, combining strawberry and vanilla vodka with some rich cream to create a tasty, filling, and—thanks to the grenadine—colorful cocktail.

INGREDIENTS

 I oz. strawberry vodka

 I oz. vanilla vodka

 2 oz. cream (to top)

 I splash of grenadine

 I fresh strawberry (garnish)

GLASSWARE

 Rocks glass

1 Pour the strawberry vodka and vanilla vodka over ice in a rocks glass. Top with the cream and stir until thoroughly mixed.

2 Finish with the splash of grenadine for color. Garnish with the fresh strawberry.

PEAR PRESSURE

We use the word "vanilla" as a code word for "bland," but that isn't quite right. It's a more subtle flavor than, say, chocolate, but that's part of what makes it great. It's definitely what makes vanilla vodka great, and one of the reasons vanilla vodka and pear go together so well. The subtlety of flavor is what separates the pear from other fruits, and pairing it with vanilla makes for an understated drink you're sure to love.

INGREDIENTS

 1 oz. vanilla vodka

 1 oz. pear juice

 1 splash of lime juice

 Sugar (for the rim)

 1 pear slice, thinly cut (garnish)

GLASSWARE
 Rocks glass

1 Add the liquid ingredients to a cocktail shaker filled with ice and shake well.

2 Rim a rocks glass with sugar and fill it with ice, and strain the contents of the cocktail shaker into it.

3 Garnish with the thin slice of pear.

QUICKSLIDE

The Mudslide is a popular cocktail, but it's a little bit complicated. The Quickslide distills this classic drink down to a simple, easy-to-make cocktail that imparts the same great flavors you've come to expect from its more involved cousin. The Quickslide is perfect for large batches, whether you're serving guests at a backyard BBQ or just looking to cool down on the beach.

INGREDIENTS

 1 oz. vodka

 1 oz. coffee liqueur

 1 oz. cream liqueur

 Ice (as needed)

 1 dusting of cocoa powder (garnish)

GLASSWARE
 Cocktail glass

1 Add the vodka, the liqueurs, and some ice to a blender. If you are using 1 oz. of each liquid ingredient, then 1 cup of ice will suffice. Note: Using more ice will create a thicker cocktail, and less ice will create a lighter cocktail.

2 Blend to the desired consistency.

3 Pour the resulting mixture into a cocktail glass.

4 Garnish with the dusting of cocoa powder.

GODMOTHER

This softer, semisweet version of the Godfather pairs perfectly with desserts as an after-dinner drink. Not unlike a fairy godmother, this drink certainly may make at least some of your dreams come true.

INGREDIENTS

 2 oz. vodka

 1 oz. amaretto

GLASSWARE

 Rocks glass

1 Place the ingredients in a rocks glass filled with crushed ice. Stir together.

BLASTOFF

Vodka cocktails are great, but sometimes you don't need an entire glass to get the job done. Shots can be a tricky thing, but when they're good, they're very good. It takes a certain amount of skill to impart enough flavor into that one gulp to make you say, "That was great!" Such is the case with the Blastoff cocktail, one swallow of which will pucker your mouth and electrify your palate.

INGREDIENTS

1 oz. vodka

½ oz. grapefruit juice

1 squeeze of lemon juice

1 squeeze of lime juice

1 orange twist (garnish)

GLASSWARE
Shot glass

1   Pour the vodka and grapefruit juice into a shot glass and finish with the quick squeeze of lemon and lime juice.

2   Garnish with the orange twist.

CHERRY SWIZZLE

Cherry lovers assemble! The blend of sweetness from the cherry vodka and sour from the lime juice and 7UP creates a perfect undertone for this cherry-tastic cocktail.

INGREDIENTS

 2 oz. Skinnygirl White Cherry vodka

 1 oz. fresh lime juice

 1 oz. 7UP Zero Sugar (to top)

GLASSWARE
Shot glasses

1 Add the cherry vodka and fresh lime juice to a cocktail shaker filled with ice. Shake vigorously for 15 to 20 seconds.

2 Strain into shot glasses, filling each glass ⅔ of the way.

3 Top with the sugar-free 7UP.

CHERRY TOOTSIE POP

The Cherry Tootsie Pop is the grown-up version of a beloved childhood treat. The addition of grenadine brings a hint of fruity flavor to this nostalgic concoction.

INGREDIENTS

 1 oz. chocolate vodka

 1 oz. Red Bull

 1 dash of grenadine

GLASSWARE
 Shot glasses

1 Combine all of the ingredients in a cocktail shaker filled with ice. Shake vigorously for 15 to 20 seconds.

2 Strain into shot glasses.

CHOCOLATE CREAM AND PEACHES

With just three simple ingredients, the Chocolate Cream and Peaches creates a medley of flavors. Slightly creamier than your average shot, this drink feels more like drinking candy.

INGREDIENTS

 1 oz. chocolate vodka

 1 oz. peach vodka

 1 oz. skim milk

GLASSWARE

 Shot glasses

1 Combine all of the ingredients in a cocktail shaker filled with ice. Shake vigorously for 15 to 20 seconds.

2 Strain into shot glasses.

GUMBALL

You can't get this out of a 25-cent machine! It's no bouncy ball or plastic ring, but you may just get the same childlike joy out of it.

INGREDIENTS

 1 oz. raspberry vodka

 1 oz. banana liqueur

 1 oz. grapefruit juice

GLASSWARE

 Shot glasses

1 Combine all of the ingredients in a cocktail shaker filled with ice. Shake vigorously for 15 to 20 seconds.

2 Strain into shot glasses.

HEAD RUSH

Everyone is going to be telling you what a great mixologist you are, but don't let it go to your head! ...Ah, what the heck, you can bask in the glory of it just a little.

INGREDIENTS

 1 oz. peach vodka

 1 oz. pear vodka

 1 oz. sambuca

GLASSWARE

 Shot glasses

1 Combine all of the ingredients in a cocktail shaker filled with ice. Shake vigorously for 15 to 20 seconds.

2 Strain into shot glasses.

JOLLY RANCHER

All the joy of a Jolly Rancher, with none of the stickiness—well, just don't spill it, and you'll be safe.

INGREDIENTS

 1 oz. apple vodka

 1 oz. cherry vodka

 1 oz. peach vodka

 1 oz. diet cranberry juice

GLASSWARE
 Shot glasses

1 Combine all of the ingredients in a cocktail shaker filled with ice. Shake vigorously for 15 to 20 seconds.

2 Strain into shot glasses.

PINK PETALS

The Pink Petals has all the delicate sweetness of a cherry blossom, with hints of vanilla to make this shot a smooth ride.

INGREDIENTS

1 oz. Skinnygirl White Cherry vodka

1 oz. Skinnygirl Island Coconut vodka

1 dash of grenadine

GLASSWARE

Shot glasses

1 Combine all of the ingredients in a cocktail shaker filled with ice. Shake vigorously for 15 to 20 seconds.

2 Strain into shot glasses.

POISON APPLE

The Poison Apple is a bit more subtle in its sweetness than the Pink Petals. With just two ingredients, this is an easy drink to make for any occasion!

INGREDIENTS

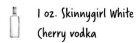 1 oz. Skinnygirl White Cherry vodka

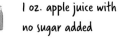 1 oz. apple juice with no sugar added

GLASSWARE
Shot glasses

1 Combine the ingredients in a cocktail shaker filled with ice. Shake vigorously for 15 to 20 seconds.

2 Strain into shot glasses.

PURPLE HOOTER

The Purple Hooter is like a perfect day, with a beautiful breeze blowing through—smooth, with just a little kick. The 7UP gives this drink a hint of bubbly fun.

INGREDIENTS

1 oz. raspberry vodka

1 oz. Skinnygirl Bare Naked vodka

1 oz. 7UP Zero Sugar, chilled (to top)

Raspberries (garnish)

GLASSWARE

Shot glasses

1 Combine the vodkas in a cocktail shaker filled with ice. Shake vigorously for 15 to 20 seconds.

2 Strain into shot glasses, filling each glass ⅔ of the way.

3 Top with the chilled sugar-free 7UP.

4 Garnish with raspberries.

STORM WARNING

You know the smell before rain? There are few things as pleasant as that smell, but this deliciously creamy shot might just have it beat.

INGREDIENTS

 1 oz. Skinnygirl White Cherry vodka

 1 oz. chocolate vodka

 1 oz. Irish cream

GLASSWARE

 Shot glasses

1 Combine all of the ingredients in a cocktail shaker filled with ice. Shake vigorously for 15 to 20 seconds.

2 Strain into shot glasses.

WOO HOO

This shot might just make you exclaim its name, once it has been drunk. Cranberry vodka introduces a subtly tart flavor to this drink, for a delicious blend!

INGREDIENTS

 3 oz. cranberry vodka

 1 oz. peach schnapps

 GLASSWARE
Shot glasses

1 Combine the ingredients in a cocktail shaker filled with ice. Shake vigorously for 15 to 20 seconds.

2 Strain into shot glasses.

ABSOLUT BITCH

Coffee lovers, this is the drink for you! There is a prominent undertone of vanilla in this drink, but the coffee liqueur and Tuaca mean that there's still plenty of that beloved coffee flavor.

INGREDIENTS

 1 oz. Absolut Vodka

 1 oz. Irish cream

 1 oz. coffee liqueur

 1 oz. Tuaca

GLASSWARE

 Shot glasses

1 Combine all of the ingredients in a cocktail shaker filled with ice. Shake vigorously for 15 to 20 seconds.

2 Strain into shot glasses.

TEDDY BEAR

You can't cuddle this shot, but you just might want to after you try it. Easy to make and easy to drink!

INGREDIENTS

 1 oz. vanilla vodka

 1 oz. root beer vodka

GLASSWARE

 Shot glasses

1 Combine the ingredients in a cocktail shaker filled with ice. Shake vigorously for 15 to 20 seconds.

2 Strain into shot glasses.

VANILLA PEAR

The Vanilla Pear is ridiculously refreshing and subtly nutty—the addition of almond extract takes this drink to the next level.

INGREDIENTS

 Sugar (for the rim)

 1 oz. pear juice

 1 oz. vanilla vodka

 1 drop of almond extract

GLASSWARE

 Shot glass

1 Wet the rim of a shot glass and then dip it into sugar.

2 Add the pear juice and vanilla vodka to a cocktail shaker filled with ice, and then add the almond extract. Shake vigorously until combined.

3 Strain into the shot glass.

ROSE SALT DOG

It may not be a familiar taste yet, but once you've tried it, you'll want it time and time again. The grapefruit juice introduces a citrusy and floral taste, with a subtly bitter aftertaste.

INGREDIENTS

 Salt (for the rim)

 2 oz. vodka

 2¼ oz. fresh grapefruit juice

 ½ oz. Giffard Crème de Pamplemousse Rose

 1 spoonful of Luxardo

 1 grapefruit slice (garnish)

 1 sprig of mint (garnish)

GLASSWARE

 Highball glass

1 Wet the rim of a highball glass and then dip it into salt.

2 Fill the glass with ice, and then add all of the remaining ingredients, except for the garnishes. Stir until combined.

3 Garnish with the grapefruit slice and mint sprig.

RUBY TWILITE

If you love lemonade, this drink should be the next one on your list! The Ruby Twilite is a tart drink, owing to the combination of grapefruit vodka and Shiner Ruby Redbird beer, which pairs deliciously with the lemonade.

INGREDIENTS

 1 oz. Deep Eddy Ruby Red Grapefruit Vodka

 4 oz. lemonade

 Shiner Ruby Redbird beer (to top)

 1 lemon wheel (garnish)

GLASSWARE
 Pint glass

1 Layer the grapefruit vodka, lemonade, and beer in a pint glass.

2 Garnish with the lemon wheel.

ROSE DE VARSOVIE

Bitter but not overbearingly so, this cocktail is classy without being pretentious. Sip this drink and picture yourself relaxing in a café on a cobblestone street.

INGREDIENTS

 1¾ oz. vodka

 ½ oz. Heering Cherry Liqueur

 4 drops of Cointreau

 3 to 4 drops of Angostura bitters

GLASSWARE

 Cocktail glass

1. Place all of the ingredients in a mixing glass filled with ice. Stir for about 15 seconds.

2. Strain into a chilled cocktail glass.

PARTY FAVORS

Vodka is a must-have spirit for any good party. Since it's such an easy liquor to pair with mixers, and it adapts so well to many kinds of flavors, it's a no-brainer when it comes to having something on hand that can satisfy a large group of guests with varied tastes. In this chapter, you'll find drinks for any and every occasion, with cocktails ranging from the Wedded Bliss to the Gingerbread.

WEDDED BLISS

While not essential, it's always nice to have a "signature cocktail" to offer guests at a wedding. You may want a cocktail specifically tailored to the theme of the wedding, but, in general, something sweet, flavorful, and slightly exotic will tantalize and excite your guests. Lychee is the perfect ingredient to do just that: it's unusual enough to spark curiosity, but familiar enough to avoid turning anyone off. The sweetness of the lychee is wedded to the sharp bite of grapefruit juice atop a vodka base, creating a blissful combination of flavors no one will object to.

INGREDIENTS

 I can or jar of lychees (with syrup)

 1 oz. vodka

 2 oz. grapefruit juice

 1 splash of lychee syrup

 2 lychees (garnish)

GLASSWARE

 Cocktail glass

1. Open the can/jar of lychees, but do not drain it. You can find lychees in syrup at most grocery stores, though you may have to look around a bit.

2. Add the vodka and grapefruit juice to a cocktail shaker filled with ice, along with a splash of the syrup from the lychees. Shake well.

3. Strain the resulting mixture into a cocktail glass. Garnish with the pair of lychees, speared with a toothpick.

RING #4

You know what's better than three? Four. The Ring #4 combines four different fruit flavors into an inviting mix that is sure to make you feel like a champion. The grenadine adds a gorgeous red color that makes this drink feel like a throwback to summer days spent sitting on the porch with a refreshing glass of raspberry lemonade. Whether you're downing these in August or February, the tasty combination of fruit flavors is sure to have you coming back for two, three, or even more—be careful!

INGREDIENTS

 1 oz. raspberry vodka

 1 splash of triple sec

 2 oz. lemonade

 1 splash of grenadine

 1 lemon slice (garnish)

GLASSWARE

 Highball glass

1 Add ice to a highball glass, and then add the raspberry vodka and triple sec.

2 Fill the rest of the glass with the lemonade and top with the splash of grenadine to add an inviting red hue to the drink.

3 Garnish with the lemon slice.

RING #5

The Ring #4 is good, but the Ring #5 is unequivocally sweeter. This is a delicious brunch cocktail that captures the feel of sangria without all the hassle. The simple addition of a handful of blueberries and raspberries gives this drink a festive red, white, and blue look when served over ice, and the fresh fruit will help you stage a comeback from even the roughest night. Let this tasty treat return you to MVP form!

INGREDIENTS

 1 handful of blueberries

 1 handful of raspberries

 1 oz. raspberry vodka

 2 oz. club soda

 1 splash of grenadine

GLASSWARE

 Highball glass

1. Add the blueberries and raspberries to a highball glass, and then fill the glass with ice.

2. Add the raspberry vodka and club soda.

3. Top with the splash of grenadine, adding more if needed to achieve the desired color.

SUMMER SPLASH

Cosmopolitans are nice, but maybe you want something a little different. A little less...pink? The Summer Splash takes a few of the best elements of the Cosmopolitan and combines them into a light, refreshing flavored lemonade. It's a citrusy take on a classic cocktail, and one that you (and the guests at your summer cookout) are sure to love.

INGREDIENTS

 1 oz. cranberry vodka

 2 oz. lemonade

 1 splash of lime juice

GLASSWARE
 Cocktail glass

1 Fill a cocktail shaker with ice and add the cranberry vodka, lemonade, and lime juice. Shake well.

2 Strain the resulting mixture into a cocktail glass.

LIQUID APPLE PIE

This drink captures what you love most about the flavor of homemade apple pie, and puts it in a glass instead of on a plate. In fact, the drink tastes so good that you might not even realize how many you've had. Much like when eating Mom's apple pie, moderation is key!

INGREDIENTS

 1 oz. vanilla vodka

 1 dash of brown sugar

 3 oz. apple cider

 1 dusting of cinnamon (garnish)

 1 cinnamon stick (garnish)

GLASSWARE

 Mason jar or glass mug

1. Add the vanilla vodka and brown sugar to a mason jar or glass mug and stir them together.

2. Pour the apple cider over the top and garnish with the dusting of cinnamon and the cinnamon stick.

VODKA SUNRISE

As beautiful as it is traditional, the Vodka Sunrise is a drink that is popular both for its tasty flavor and gorgeous hues. Its appearance lives up to its name—the cocktail looks like nothing so much as the sun rising over the horizon in the morning, with reds, oranges, and yellows playing off one another in a fantastic medley of color.

INGREDIENTS

 I oz. vodka

 I dash of lemon juice

 2 oz. orange juice

 I splash of grenadine

 I orange slice (garnish)

GLASSWARE

 Highball glass

1 Add ice to a highball glass, and then pour in the vodka and lemon juice. Mix together.

2 Add the orange juice to fill, then top with the splash of grenadine. Rather than stirring, allow the grenadine to slowly filter down through the orange juice and vodka.

3 Garnish with the orange slice.

DRINK THE C

C is for Cointreau, that's good enough for me. But it helps to have a few more flavors in there, like cherry vodka, coconut rum, and cola, to round out the flavor profile of this C-heavy concoction. Is it a bit contrived for the sake of its name? Maybe. But it's also a delicious combination of flavors with a simple cola base, making this a simple, straightforward, and tasty cocktail fit for any occasion.

INGREDIENTS

 1 oz. cherry vodka

 2 oz. Coca-Cola

 1 splash of coconut rum

 1 splash of Cointreau

 1 maraschino cherry (garnish)

GLASSWARE

 Rocks glass

1 Add ice, the cherry vodka, and the Coca-Cola to a rocks glass and stir together.

2 Top with the splash of coconut rum and Cointreau and stir again.

3 Garnish with the maraschino cherry.

BUTTERBREW

What do you crave during a movie night? How about something that mimics the rich, buttery flavor of movie theater popcorn? Butterscotch schnapps does just that, adding a playful element alongside a classic cream soda base. With vanilla vodka mixed in, it's a complex cocktail that unifies disparate flavors into a surprisingly cohesive whole. The Butterbrew is exactly what you're looking for while enjoying a casual movie night at home.

INGREDIENTS

 1 oz. vanilla vodka

 1 oz. butterscotch schnapps

 4 oz. cream soda (to top)

GLASSWARE

 Highball glass

1. Add the vanilla vodka and butterscotch schnapps to a cocktail shaker filled with ice. Shake well.

2. Strain the resulting mixture into a highball glass filled with ice.

3. Top with the cream soda.

CAPE COD

Perfect for dinner parties or holiday festivities in any season, this iconic drink is an easy addition to your next get-together.

INGREDIENTS

 1½ oz. vodka

 5 oz. cranberry juice

 1 lime wedge (garnish)

GLASSWARE
Highball glass

1 Build in a chilled highball glass filled with ice cubes.

2 Garnish with the lime wedge.

GINGERBREAD

Gingerbread automatically makes one feel festive. There are few flavors that represent the winter holidays quite so strongly, and few drinks that utilize it quite so well.

INGREDIENTS

 I oz. RumChata

 I oz. Domaine de Canton

 I oz. vanilla vodka

GLASSWARE
 Shot glasses

1 Combine all of the ingredients in a cocktail shaker filled with ice. Shake vigorously for 15 to 20 seconds.

2 Strain into shot glasses.

ANGEL'S KISS

Whether you're sharing a shot with your sweetheart, celebrating love of all kinds with your pals, or investing in some quality time with yourself, this drink will make you feel all warm and fuzzy.

INGREDIENTS

 1 oz. chocolate vodka

 1 oz. skim milk

 3 drops of grenadine

GLASSWARE
Shot glass

1 Fill a shot glass halfway with the chocolate vodka.

2 Place a barspoon upside down just barely above the vodka, touching the side of the glass.

3 Slowly and carefully pour the skim milk over the spoon and into the glass until the glass is full.

4 Carefully add the drops of grenadine into the center of the milk layer.

HELL'S GATE

No summer celebration is complete without this concoction. The heat of the Tabasco and wasabi paste is cooled by the cucumber vodka, for a shot that's smooth but still packs a punch.

INGREDIENTS

 1 oz. Skinnygirl Cucumber vodka

 3 to 4 drops of Tabasco

 1 dash of wasabi paste

 1 thin slice of cucumber (garnish)

GLASSWARE
Shot glass

1 Combine all of the ingredients in a cocktail shaker filled with ice. Shake vigorously for 15 to 20 seconds.

2 Strain into a shot glass.

3 Garnish with the thin slice of cucumber.

CHOCO PEAT

Looking to spice up your Valentine's Day, your anniversary, or just a regular date night? The Choco Peat brings the heat with spicy vodka, tempered by the sweetness of chocolate liqueur. The Kahlúa added to this drink introduces a coffee taste to even everything out.

INGREDIENTS

 ½ oz. dark chocolate liqueur

 ¾ oz. Kahlúa

 1¼ oz. Stolichnaya Stoli Hot vodka (or other spicy vodka)

 ¾ oz. The Peat Monster whisky

 GLASSWARE
Cocktail glass

1 Place all of the ingredients in a mixing glass filled with ice, stir, and strain into a cocktail glass.

BONA DEA

When enjoying an elegant evening, the Bona Dea is the perfect drink to impress your guests. The carbonation of the sparkling wine makes any occasion feel special.

INGREDIENTS

 1 oz. peach vodka

 1 oz. cranberry juice

 Sparkling wine (to top)

 1 lemon twist (garnish)

GLASSWARE
 Rocks glass

1 Combine the peach vodka and cranberry juice in a rocks glass filled with ice and stir.

2 Top with sparkling wine and garnish with the lemon twist.

JUNGLE PUNCH

Fruit punch has never been so fun. While thought of as a summer staple, there's no rule that says the Jungle Punch can't be just as satisfying in any season.

INGREDIENTS

 1 oz. vodka

 1 oz. Sprite

 3 oz. fruit punch

GLASSWARE

 Pitcher or punch bowl

1   Combine the vodka, Sprite, and fruit punch in a pitcher or punch bowl filled with ice. Stir until thoroughly mixed.

BISOUS DU SOLEIL

Meaning "kisses from the sun," this drink will make you forgive the sun for making it so hot and miserable in the height of summertime. The subtle taste of orange adds a citrusy undertone to this tasty drink.

INGREDIENTS

 1 oz. vodka

 1 dash of Cointreau

 1½ oz. cranberry juice

 Juice of ½ lime

 Juice of 1 orange wedge

 Champagne (to top)

GLASSWARE

 Champagne flute

1 Add the vodka, Cointreau, and juices to a cocktail shaker filled with ice. Shake vigorously.

2 Strain into a Champagne flute. Top with Champagne.

MR. FUNK

Mr. Funk is the life of the party. The host with the most. The secret sauce! Add it to the mix and see what happens.

INGREDIENTS

 1 oz. peach vodka

 1 oz. cranberry juice

 Sparkling wine (to top)

 1 lemon twist (garnish)

 GLASSWARE

Champagne glass

1 Place the peach vodka and cranberry juice in a Champagne glass. Stir together.

2 Top with sparkling wine.

3 Garnish with the lemon twist.

AMELIA

This treat is best enjoyed when you have access to fresh blackberries; in North America, that means summertime. This recipe includes fresh blackberry puree, which adds a deep, rich flavor to this drink.

INGREDIENTS

 1½ oz. vodka

 1 oz. Blackberry Puree (included recipe)

 ¾ oz. St-Germain

 ½ oz. fresh lemon juice

 1 sprig of mint (garnish)

 Blackberries (garnish)

GLASSWARE
 Cocktail glass

1 Pour the vodka, puree, St-Germain, and fresh lemon juice into a cocktail shaker. Add large ice cubes, shake vigorously, and strain into a chilled cocktail glass.

2 Garnish with the mint sprig and blackberries.

BLACKBERRY PUREE RECIPE:

1 cup blackberries (fresh or thawed)

2 tablespoons caster sugar

2 tablespoons water

2 tablespoons fresh lemon juice

1 Combine all of the ingredients in a blender and puree until smooth.

2 Strain and store in the refrigerator for up to 4 days. Makes about 1 cup.

SWEET AND SOURS

The mix of sweet and sour is a long-beloved contradictory combination. At first blush, putting two opposite flavors together sounds like a terrible idea, but as we've likely all learned, sometimes opposites attract in the very best way. This chapter is full of drinks that celebrate sweet sipping that might also make your face pucker. The Appletini, Blue Lagoon, and Pink Lemonade are all perfect ways to shake things up a little bit.

BLUE FIREFLIES

The Blue Fireflies is a delicious cocktail that changes as you drink it. The primary flavors at play here are vodka, lemon, and lime, but as the blue curaçao ice cubes melt, the drink takes on a blue hue and a bit of orange flavor begins to seep in. This gives the cocktail an alluring, transformative quality.

INGREDIENTS

 3 blue curaçao ice cubes

 1 oz. vodka

 2 oz. Sprite

 1 splash of fresh lime juice

 1 strip of orange peel (garnish)

GLASSWARE

 Highball glass

1 Make ice cubes using blue curaçao.

2 Add three blue curaçao ice cubes to a highball glass.

3 Add the vodka, Sprite, and fresh lime juice.

4 Stir together and garnish with the strip of orange peel.

VODKA GIMLET

Lime is usually associated with tequila, but it's an underrated partner to vodka! You'd be surprised at how such simple ingredients create such a satisfying cocktail.

INGREDIENTS

 1 ½ oz. vodka

 ½ oz. fresh lime juice

 1 lime wheel (garnish)

GLASSWARE

 Cocktail glass

1. Place the vodka and fresh lime juice in a mixing glass filled with ice and strain into a cocktail glass.

2. Garnish with the lime wheel.

KAMIKAZE

This classic cocktail represents the perfect balance between sugar and acidity, creating a delicious sweet-and-sour drink! The Kamikaze can also be a tasty shot, depending on personal preference.

INGREDIENTS

 I oz. vodka

 ¼ oz. triple sec

 1.4 oz. lime juice

 I lime twist (garnish)

GLASSWARE
 Cocktail glass or shot glasses

1 Place all of the ingredients, except for the garnish in a mixing glass filled with ice. Stir to combine.

2 Strain, garnish with the lime twist, and serve in a cocktail glass or shot glass.

A LITTLE LEM

Two parts vodka, one part lemon juice, one part blueberry liqueur. Aside from a basic, two-ingredient Martini, it doesn't get much simpler than that. But this straightforward cocktail packs a real wallop of flavor, balancing the tartness of the lemon against the sweetness of the blueberry atop a foundation of vodka. A sprig of mint gives it a slightly herbaceous quality, adding the faintest hint of yet another flavor profile to give this simple cocktail a surprising amount of depth.

INGREDIENTS

 2 oz. vodka

 1 oz. blueberry liqueur

 1 oz. lemon juice

 1 small handful of blueberries (garnish)

 1 lemon wedge (garnish)

 1 sprig of mint (garnish)

GLASSWARE
Rocks glass

1 Add the vodka, blueberry liqueur, and lemon juice to a cocktail shaker filled with ice. Shake well.

2 Strain the resulting mixture into a rocks glass. Add the desired amount of ice.

3 Garnish with the small handful of blueberries, lemon wedge, and sprig of mint.

APPLETINI

What was your favorite candy flavor growing up? If you liked the taste of sour apple, this Martini might just be your new favorite!

INGREDIENTS

 3 oz. vodka

 1 oz. DeKuyper Sour Apple Pucker

 1 oz. triple sec

 2 thin slices of apple (garnish)

GLASSWARE
 Cocktail glass

1　Add the vodka, Sour Apple Pucker, and triple sec to a cocktail shaker filled with ice and shake vigorously.

2　Strain the resulting mixture into a cocktail glass.

3　Garnish with the thin slices of apple.

BLUE LAGOON

Similar to the Lemonade Shocker, the Blue Lagoon is vibrant in color and delivers a sweet twist. The addition of maraschino cherries adds to the festive feeling of the drink, making it ideal for patriotic celebrations!

INGREDIENTS

 1 oz. vodka

 1 oz. blue curaçao

 4 oz. lemonade (to top)

 1 splash of lime juice

 1 lemon wheel (garnish)

 1 maraschino cherry (garnish)

GLASSWARE

 Mason jar

1. Add the vodka and blue curaçao to a cocktail shaker filled with ice. Shake vigorously.

2. Place the desired amount of ice in a mason jar and strain the mixture into it.

3. Top with the lemonade and splash of lime juice.

4. Garnish with the lemon wheel and maraschino cherry.

CITRUS SUNSET

If you're a fan of the Tequila Sunrise, the Citrus Sunset might just be the vodka equivalent you've been searching for. Beautiful and full of flavor, this drink is a guaranteed hit.

INGREDIENTS

 1 oz. vodka

 4 oz. grapefruit juice

 Juice of ½ lime

 Juice of ¼ lemon

 1 dash of grenadine

 1 cherry (garnish)

GLASSWARE

 Mason jar

1 Place the desired amount of ice in a mason jar, and then add the vodka and grapefruit juice. Add the lime juice and lemon juice. Stir until mixed.

2 Pour the dash of grenadine into the middle of the drink and allow it to sink to the bottom, creating a subtle layering effect with the grapefruit juice.

3 Garnish with the cherry.

GRAPE SOURBALL

A warm-weather treat, this drink takes a sour twist on the Grape Chill (see page 79). Fresh, fruity, and fabulous!

INGREDIENTS

 1 oz. grape vodka

 1 oz. Crystal Light Lemonade

 1 oz. orange juice

 Orange slices (garnish)

GLASSWARE

Shot glasses, rocks glass, or cocktail glass

1   Combine all of the ingredients, except for the garnish, in a cocktail shaker filled with ice. Shake vigorously for 15 to 20 seconds.

2   Strain into shot glasses and garnish with the orange slices. Alternatively, serve on the rocks or in a cocktail glass.

GREAT IDEA

Jägermeister and lemon? Great Idea! Why didn't we think of it sooner?

INGREDIENTS

 1 oz. vodka

 1 oz. Jägermeister

 ½ oz. lemon juice

 1 lemon wedge (garnish)

GLASSWARE

Highball glass

1 Combine all of the ingredients in a highball glass and gently stir.

2 Fill the glass with ice.

3 Garnish with the lemon wedge.

CHILTON

This drink is simplicity itself. There's plenty of room to focus on the great taste of your vodka and lemon juice—a classic combo.

INGREDIENTS

 Salt (for the rim)

 1½ oz. vodka

 Juice of 2 lemons

 Topo Chico (to top)

 1 lemon wheel (garnish)

GLASSWARE
 Highball glass

1 Wet the rim of a highball glass and then dip it into salt.

2 Fill the glass with ice, add the vodka and lemon juice, and top with Topo Chico. Stir together.

3 Garnish with the lemon wheel.

VINEYARD SPLASH

When temperatures rise, you'll need a refreshing drink to quench your thirst, cool you down, and motivate you to keep enjoying the day despite the heat! Luckily, the Vineyard Splash is up to the challenge.

INGREDIENTS

 1 oz. purple-grape-and-watermelon puree

 1 teaspoon sugar (plus more for the rim)

 Juice of ½ lime

 1 oz. vodka

 1 dash of club soda

 1 handful of watermelon cubes (garnish)

GLASSWARE

 Mason jar

1. If making the puree from scratch, place 4 oz. of fresh purple grapes in a food processor, along with the juice from half of a lime. Add ¼ cup of fresh watermelon and blend until smooth.

2. Wet the rim of a mason jar, dip it into some sugar, and add the desired amount of ice.

3. Add the lime juice and vodka and pour in the puree. Add the sugar and stir thoroughly.

4. Top with the dash of club soda and garnish with the watermelon cubes, skewered on a toothpick.

BERRIES FROM THE WEST

If you've ever had blueberry lemonade, you'll know why this combination works so well. Plus, nothing says summer like blueberries and lemonade!

INGREDIENTS

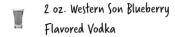 2 oz. Western Son Blueberry Flavored Vodka

1 oz. Simple Syrup (see page 7)

1 oz. fresh lemon juice

1 lemon wheel (garnish)

Blueberries (garnish)

GLASSWARE

Rocks glass

1 Combine all of the ingredients in a cocktail shaker filled with ice. Shake vigorously.

2 Strain into a rocks glass filled with ice.

3 Garnish with the lemon wheel and blueberries.

RASPBERRY TWIST

The Raspberry Twist is an alcoholic twist on an AriZona Raspberry Half & Half. This refreshing drink is perfect for sitting out by the pool on a hot day!

INGREDIENTS

 1 oz. raspberry vodka

 2 oz. lemonade

 2 oz. sweetened iced tea

 3 to 4 raspberries (garnish)

 3 to 4 lemon wheels (garnish)

GLASSWARE

 Mason jar

1 Place the desired amount of ice in a mason jar and add the raspberry vodka.

2 Add the lemonade and sweetened iced tea. Stir until thoroughly mixed.

3 Garnish with the raspberries and lemon wheels.

PINK PANTHER

The sparkling lemonade elevates it and classes up this sweet-and-sour citrus drink, making it great for all occasions, from dinner parties to cookouts.

INGREDIENTS

 2 oz. Grey Goose Vodka

 1 oz. St-Germain

 Juice from ½ grapefruit

 Juice from ½ lime

 Juice from ½ lemon

 1 cherry

 Sparkling French Berry Lemonade (to top)

 Lime wedges (garnish)

 Raspberries (garnish)

GLASSWARE
Highball glass

1. Combine all of the ingredients, except for the lemonade and garnishes, in a cocktail shaker filled with ice. Shake vigorously.

2. Strain into a highball glass filled with ice.

3. Top with lemonade and garnish with the lime wedges and raspberries.

PINK LEMONADE

Regular lemonade is nice, but pink lemonade just has a certain je ne sais quoi! This buzzy version is a guaranteed hit.

INGREDIENTS

 2 oz. vodka

 2 oz. lemon juice

 2 oz. diet cranberry juice

 1 lemon wheel (garnish)

GLASSWARE

 Mason jar

1　Combine all of the ingredients in a cocktail shaker filled with ice. Shake vigorously for 15 to 20 seconds.

2　Strain into a mason jar and garnish with the lemon wheel.

LEMONADE SHOCKER

A bright twist on a simple lemonade, the Lemonade Shocker is best known for its bright blue color. The addition of blue curaçao is to thank for its vibrant appearance!

INGREDIENTS

 2 oz. vodka

 1 oz. blue curaçao

 2 oz. lemon juice

 2 oz. club soda (to top)

 1 lemon slice (garnish)

 3 lime slices (garnish)

GLASSWARE

 Mason jar

1 Place the desired amount of ice in a mason jar.

2 Add the vodka, blue curaçao, and lemon juice and stir.

3 Top with the club soda and garnish with the lemon and lime slices..

LEMON DROP

This drink is almost as iconic as lemonade itself. Simple and classic, this is as good as anything you'd order out. We recommend wetting the rim with one of the spent lemons.

INGREDIENTS

 2 oz. vodka

 1 oz. triple sec

 1 oz. lemon juice

 Sugar (for the rim)

 1 lemon twist (garnish)

 ### GLASSWARE
Cocktail glass

1. Add the vodka, triple sec, and lemon juice to a cocktail shaker filled with ice. Shake vigorously.

2. Wet the rim of a cocktail glass and then dip it into sugar.

3. Strain the cocktail into the glass.

4. Garnish with the twist of lemon.

COFFEE CONCOCTIONS

Coffee and alcohol is another combination that isn't exactly intuitive, but if you think about it, it makes perfect sense. These cocktails are ideal for those of us who sometimes get a bit sleepy when we drink—no shame, but sometimes it's nice to have a little something else to keep the party going. And no spirit pairs better with coffee than vodka. With delicious drinks like the White Russian, Espresso Martini, and Mason Jar Mudslide, it's no wonder the coffee-and-vodka combination gets its own chapter in this book.

WHITE RUSSIAN

What could be better than a White Russian? This simple mixture of vodka, coffee liqueur, and cream provides a rich, delicious, and refreshing flavor that is perfect for summer and winter alike!

INGREDIENTS

 1 oz. vodka

 1 oz. coffee liqueur

 2 oz. cream

GLASSWARE

 Rocks glass

1 Fill a rocks glass with ice and add the vodka and coffee liqueur.

2 Slowly pour the cream over the vodka mixture.

3 Stir the ingredients together slowly.

CLASSIC WHITE RUSSIAN

Let's get the word "Russian" out of the way first: this drink's connection to Russia is the vodka. It wasn't created in Russia or by a Russian. And the White Russian cannot be discussed without first examining the Black Russian, a vodka-and-Kahlúa cocktail supposedly created in the late 1940s by bartender Gustave Tops in Brussels at the Hotel Metropole, in honor of the American ambassador to Luxembourg, Perle Mesta. The Oklahoma-born Mesta was a politically active socialite. Her support for Harry S. Truman's two presidential campaigns secured her overseas appointment and laid the foundation for the Irving Berlin musical *Call Me Madam*, starring Ethel Merman as a character largely based on Mesta. Neither the play nor the history books document who added the cream to concoct the White Russian, though the cocktail's first known appearance in print can be traced back to 1965 ads for a coffee liqueur.

INGREDIENTS

 1½ oz. vodka

 ½ oz. Kahlúa

 1 dash of cream

GLASSWARE

 Rocks glass

1 Add the vodka and Kahlúa to a rocks glass filled with ice. Stir together.

2 Top with the dash of cream.

FANCY WHITE RUSSIAN

There's nothing better than a cinnamon latte on a cold winter day to embrace the holiday season. The Fancy White Russian is a vodka rendition of the latte, perfect for holiday get-togethers throughout the fall and winter.

INGREDIENTS

 1 oz. vodka

 1 oz. coffee liqueur

 3 oz. milk

 Dusting of nutmeg (garnish)

 1 cinnamon stick (garnish)

GLASSWARE

 Rocks glass

1 Add the vodka, coffee liqueur, and milk to a cocktail shaker filled with ice. Shake vigorously.

2 Place ice in a rocks glass and strain the contents of the shaker into it.

3 Garnish with the dusting of nutmeg and the cinnamon stick.

MOCHA MOCHA MOCHA

Beware: this is a drink as dangerous as any out there. It is a mixture of sweet flavors so delicious that you're likely to forget that you're drinking something extremely strong. With three out of four ingredients containing alcohol, it's the sort of drink that might put you on the floor before you realize what's happened. Still, if flavor is what's most important (and we maintain that it is!), you won't do much better than this fantastic concoction.

INGREDIENTS

 1 oz. vodka

 1 oz. chocolate liqueur

 1 oz. coffee liqueur

 2 oz. milk

GLASSWARE

 Rocks glass

1 Add the vodka, liqueurs, and milk to a cocktail shaker filled with ice and shake vigorously.

2 Strain the resulting mixture into a rocks glass filled with ice.

MIND ERASER

Coffee lovers can't get enough of the Mind Eraser! The lingering taste of hazelnut and coffee leaves only hints of the vodka behind. Beware: this potent cocktail is known to live up to its name!

INGREDIENTS

 ³/₄ oz. coffee liqueur

 ³/₄ oz. vodka

 ³/₄ oz. tonic water

GLASSWARE

 Double shot glass

1 Layer in a double shot glass.

2 Drink through a straw.

ESPRESSO MARTINI

If you are a fan of the Mind Eraser (see page 223), you will surely love this drink too! If you're not a fan of the Mind Eraser but you like coffee, consider this the ideal alternative.

INGREDIENTS

 3 oz. vodka

 1 oz. Kahlúa

 2 oz. espresso

 1 handful of espresso beans (garnish)

GLASSWARE

 Coupe

1 Add the vodka, Kahlúa, and espresso to a cocktail shaker filled with ice. Shake vigorously.

2 Strain the resulting mixture into a coupe.

3 Garnish with the espresso beans.

DEEP THROAT

Here's another drink with coffee undertones, for those who can't get enough of the rich, bitter flavor! The Deep Throat is topped with whipped cream, creating a cozy concoction for nights in.

INGREDIENTS

 1 oz. coffee vodka

 1 oz. whipped cream vodka

 1 dollop of whipped cream (to top)

GLASSWARE
 Shot glasses

1 Add the coffee vodka and whipped cream vodka to a cocktail shaker filled with ice. Shake vigorously for 15 to 20 seconds.

2 Strain into shot glasses and top with the whipped cream. Drink without using your hands.

DANGEROUS GRANDMA

Woody, nutty, and citrusy flavors all meet here to create a delicious drink. The addition of coffee vodka provides an extra boost of flavor that pairs perfectly with the richness of this drink.

INGREDIENTS

 1 oz. coffee vodka

 1 oz. whiskey

 1 oz. amaretto

 1 oz. orange juice

GLASSWARE

 Rocks glass

1 Combine all of the ingredients in a cocktail shaker filled with ice. Shake vigorously for 15 to 20 seconds.

2 Strain into a rocks glass.

MASON JAR MUDSLIDE

The Mason Jar Mudslide is a deliciously creamy, rich drink, made for those with a sweet tooth! Whip it up in big batches for holiday festivities or more laid-back get-togethers with your friends and family.

INGREDIENTS

 I oz. vodka

 I oz. coffee liqueur

 I oz. Irish cream

 I oz. heavy cream

 I cup ice

 Chocolate syrup (as needed)

 I dollop of whipped cream (to top)

 Caramel syrup (garnish)

 Cinnamon sticks (garnish)

GLASSWARE

Mason jar

1 Place the vodka, coffee liqueur, Irish cream, heavy cream, and ice in a blender. (For added chocolaty taste, add a dash of chocolate syrup to the blender before pureeing.) Puree until the desired consistency is achieved.

2 Pour the cocktail into a mason jar. Top with the whipped cream and drizzle chocolate syrup on top.

3 Garnish with caramel syrup and cinnamon sticks.

MAGNIFICENT MARTINIS

For many people, when they think vodka, they think Martinis. Martinis are a staple of the cocktail world, and though you can make a Martini without vodka, why would you? There's a reason that this is such an iconic subgenre of vodka drinks. Whether you want to keep things simple with the Classic Vodka Martini or spice them up with something like the Bellini Martini or Birthday Martini, rest assured that there is a Martini in this chapter for you.

CLASSIC VODKA MARTINI

Arguably the most recognizable vodka cocktail, you can never go wrong with the Classic Vodka Martini.

INGREDIENTS

 2 oz. Skyy Vodka

 ½ oz. dry vermouth

 1 lemon twist (garnish)

GLASSWARE
 Cocktail glass

1 Place the vodka and vermouth in a mixing glass filled with ice and stir until thoroughly combined.

2 Strain the resulting mixture into a cocktail glass.

3 Garnish with the twist of lemon.

BUDGET VODKA MARTINI

In need of a quick, low-cost drink that'll still impress? The Budget Vodka Martini will be your savior!

INGREDIENTS

 1 oz. Svedka Vodka

 1 oz. dry vermouth

 1 dash of lemon juice

 Olives, skewered (garnish)

GLASSWARE

 Cocktail glass

1. Place the vodka, vermouth, and lemon juice in a mixing glass filled with ice.

2. Stir until thoroughly combined and strain the resulting mixture into a cocktail glass. Garnish with skewered olives.

PURIST'S VODKA MARTINI

If you are looking for a simple drink where vodka is the star of the show, the Purist's Vodka Martini is the drink for you!

INGREDIENTS

 2 drops of dry vermouth

 1¾ oz. vodka

 olives, skewered (garnish)

GLASSWARE

 Cocktail glass

1 Place the vermouth in a cocktail shaker filled with ice and add the vodka. Stir or shake.

2 Strain into a chilled cocktail glass and garnish with skewered olives.

DRY VODKA MARTINI

The Dry Vodka Martini is ideal for those looking for a vodka-heavy cocktail. With just two ingredients (and a garnish), this drink is a simple and easy play on the classic!

INGREDIENTS

 2 oz. vodka

 ¼ oz. dry vermouth

 1 lemon twist (garnish)

GLASSWARE

 Cocktail glass

1. Place the vodka and vermouth in a mixing glass filled with ice and stir until thoroughly combined.

2. Strain the resulting mixture into a cocktail glass and garnish with the twist of lemon.

WET VODKA MARTINI

If you want a Vodka Martini that's a little less intense, the Wet Vodka Martini is it! Though it's made with the same simple ingredients, the ratio difference means that this drink will be slightly milder in taste.

INGREDIENTS

 2 oz. vodka

 1 oz. dry vermouth

 1 lime twist (garnish)

GLASSWARE
 Cocktail glass

1 Place the vodka and vermouth in a mixing glass filled with ice and stir until thoroughly combined.

2 Strain the resulting mixture into a cocktail glass and garnish with the twist of lime.

PERFECT VODKA MARTINI

Need a little more sweetness in your Martini? The Perfect Vodka Martini is just what it says it is: perfect! The notes of cocoa, caramel, and vanilla within the sweet vermouth will soften up this cocktail to be just right.

INGREDIENTS

 2 oz. vodka

 ½ oz. dry vermouth

 ½ oz. sweet vermouth

 1 lemon twist (garnish)

GLASSWARE

 Cocktail glass

1   Place the vodka and vermouths in a mixing glass filled with ice and stir until thoroughly combined.

2   Strain the resulting mixture into a cocktail glass and garnish with the twist of lemon.

DIRTY VODKA MARTINI

The Dirty Vodka Martini is similar to The Dirty Spy (see page 49), with a bit more emphasis on the vodka.

INGREDIENTS

 2 oz. vodka

 ½ oz. dry vermouth

 1 splash of olive brine

 3 pimento-stuffed olives (garnish)

GLASSWARE
 Cocktail glass

1 Place the vodka, vermouth, and olive brine in a mixing glass filled with ice. Stir thoroughly.

2 Strain the resulting mixture into a cocktail glass and garnish with the pimento-stuffed olives, skewered on a toothpick.

BELLINI MARTINI

This delicious medley of vodka, peach schnapps, and Champagne is sure to please! The peach slice is the figurative cherry on top of this already scrumptious drink.

INGREDIENTS

 2 oz. vodka

 1 oz. peach schnapps

 1 splash of Simple Syrup (see page 7)

 1 oz. Champagne

 1 peach slice (garnish)

GLASSWARE

 Cocktail glass

1. Add the vodka, peach schnapps, and Simple Syrup to a cocktail shaker filled with ice. Shake vigorously.

2. Place the Champagne in the cocktail shaker and gently stir.

3. Strain the resulting mixture into a cocktail glass.

4. Garnish with the slice of peach.

BIRTHDAY MARTINI

When you're in a playful mood, chances are you don't want to slowly sip an aged whiskey and try to pick out the different flavor notes. You want something fun! And probably something sweet too. The Birthday Martini delivers on both counts, providing a fresh take on a classic recipe and offering a rich mixture of vanilla, chocolate, and amaretto flavors. Rimming the glass with sprinkles really adds to the playful vibe.

INGREDIENTS

 Colorful sprinkles (for the rim)

 2 oz. vanilla vodka

 2 oz. heavy cream

 1 oz. white chocolate liqueur

 1 splash of amaretto

 GLASSWARE
Cocktail glass

1. Wet the rim of a cocktail glass and press it into colorful sprinkles.

2. Combine the liquid ingredients in a cocktail shaker filled with ice. Shake well.

3. Strain the resulting mixture into the cocktail glass.

RASPBERRY MARTINI

The tartness of raspberries mixes deliciously with the sweetness of Simple Syrup and triple sec. This spin gives the Raspberry Martini a fruity touch without making it too sugary sweet.

INGREDIENTS

 8 raspberries
(3 of them for garnish)

 1 splash of Simple Syrup
(see page 7)

 2 oz. raspberry vodka

 1 oz. triple sec

GLASSWARE

 Cocktail glass

1. At the bottom of a cocktail shaker, muddle 5 of the raspberries and the Simple Syrup.

2. Add ice, the raspberry vodka, and the triple sec. Shake vigorously.

3. Strain the resulting mixture into a cocktail glass.

4. Garnish with 3 of the raspberries.

SOUR CHERRY MARTINI

The Sour Cherry Martini puts a tangy twist on a Dirty Shirley! The punch from the lime juice is just what's needed to balance out the cherry and grenadine.

INGREDIENTS

 1 oz. vodka

 2 oz. cherry vodka

 1 oz. lime juice

 1 dash of grenadine

 1 lime twist (garnish)

 2 maraschino cherries (garnish)

GLASSWARE

 Cocktail glass

1 Add the vodka, cherry vodka, lime juice, and grenadine to a cocktail shaker filled with ice. Shake vigorously.

2 Strain the resulting mixture into a cocktail glass.

3 Garnish with the lime twist and maraschino cherries.

FRENCH MARTINI DE NANCY

Imagine sitting in a café by the Eiffel Tower on a sunny (but not too hot!) day, as fashionable locals breeze by you. This is the exact drink you would want in your hand. Drink it and let it transport you!

INGREDIENTS

 ½ oz. Giffard Crème de Pamplemousse Rose

 1½ oz. vodka

 2 oz. grapefruit juice

 1 squeeze of lemon juice

GLASSWARE

 Cocktail glass

1 Combine all of the ingredients in a cocktail shaker filled with ice and shake vigorously.

2 Strain into a cocktail glass.

VESPER MARTINI

The Vesper Martini is quite sweet in flavor, thanks to the gin and Lillet Blanc. Both ingredients add a subtly herbal and fruity edge to this drink.

INGREDIENTS

 1 oz. vodka

 3 oz. gin

 ½ oz. Lillet Blanc

 1 lemon twist (garnish)

 GLASSWARE
Cocktail glass

1 Add the vodka, gin, and Lillet Blanc to a cocktail shaker filled with ice. Shake well.

2 Strain into a cocktail glass.

3 Garnish with the lemon twist.

SPICY MARTINI

If you want to spice up your evening—pun intended—this is the way to do it. The hot sauce and jalapeño-stuffed olives create a thrilling, fiery flavor.

INGREDIENTS

 2 oz. vodka

 ½ oz. dry vermouth

 1 dash of jalapeño pepper hot sauce

 2 jalapeño-stuffed olives (garnish)

 GLASSWARE
Cocktail glass

1 Add the vodka, vermouth, and hot sauce to a cocktail shaker filled with ice. Shake vigorously.

2 Strain the resulting mixture into a cocktail glass.

3 Garnish with the jalapeño-stuffed olives, skewered on a toothpick.

MCCLURE'S PICKLE MARTINI

For all the pickle fans in search of a satisfactory Martini, the McClure's Pickle Martini will end your quest for the perfectly salty drink!

INGREDIENTS

 2 oz. vodka

 1 oz. brine from a jar of McClure's Pickles

 3 pickle slices (garnish)

GLASSWARE
 Cocktail glass

1 Place the vodka and brine in a mixing glass filled with ice.

2 Stir until very cold, and then strain into a chilled cocktail glass.

3 Garnish with the pickle slices.

PICKLED MARTINI

If you're a fan of the McClure's Pickle Martini (see page 262), then you will love the Pickled Martini. Although they are quite similar in flavor, vodka is slightly more prominent in the Pickled Martini, and it also features the addition of dry vermouth. The tart, sweet taste of cornichons is a pleasant accessory to this drink.

INGREDIENTS

 2 oz. vodka

 ½ oz. dry vermouth

 1 splash of pickle juice

 1 to 2 cornichons (garnish)

GLASSWARE
 Cocktail glass

1   Place the vodka, vermouth, and pickle juice in a mixing glass filled with ice. Stir until thoroughly combined.

2   Strain the resulting mixture into a cocktail glass.

3   Garnish with 1 to 2 cornichons, skewered on a toothpick.

INDEX

Absolut Bitch recipe, 126
Absolut vodka, Absolut Bitch, 126
amaretto
    Birthday Martini, 250
    Dangerous Grandma, 228
    Godmother, 101
    The Slammer, 83
Amelia recipe, 175
Angel's Kiss recipe, 160
Angostura bitters, Rose de Varsovie, 137
Aperol, 100% Vitamin Water, 84
apple vodka, Jolly Rancher, 114
apples/apple juice
    Appletini, 186
    Poison Apple, 118
Appletini recipe, 186

bacon, Mason Jar Bloody Mary, 46
bar tools, 5
Bellini Martini recipe, 249
Berezinski, Sophie, 37
Berries From the West recipe, 201
Betty's Cosmo recipe, 60
Birthday Martini recipe, 250
Bisous du Soleil recipe, 171
The Bitter End Memphis Barbecue Bitters, The Incredible Apicius Bloody Mary, 42
black pepper
    The Incredible Apicius Bloody Mary, 42
    Mason Jar Bloody Mary, 46
    The Original Bloody Mary, 45
Black Russian, 216
blackberries
    Amelia, 175
    Blackberry Puree, 175
Blackberry Puree recipe, 175
Blastoff recipe, 102
blue curaçao
    Blue Fireflies, 178
    Blue Lagoon, 189

Herbal Affirmation, 88
    Lemonade Shocker, 209
Blue Fireflies recipe, 178
Blue Lagoon recipe, 189
blueberries
    Berries From the West, 201
    A Little Lem, 185
    Ring #5, 144
blueberry liqueur, A Little Lem, 185
Bona Dea recipe, 167
Bond, James, 49
Borrowed Thyme recipe, 56
bowl, 100% Vitamin Water, 84
Budget Cosmopolitan recipe, 21
Budget Vodka Martini recipe, 237
Butterbrew recipe, 155
butterscotch schnapps, Butterbrew, 155
By the Horns recipe, 59

Call Me Madam (musical), 216
Campari
    Sunny Day, 87
    Vodka Negroni, 14
Candy-Coated Nostalgia
    Creamsicle, 93
    Strawberries and Cream, 94
Cape Cod recipe, 156
Capescrew recipe, 34
carafe, 100% Vitamin Water, 84
celery bitters/celery salt
    The Incredible Apicius Bloody Mary, 42
    Mason Jar Bloody Mary, 46
    100% Vitamin Water, 84
Champagne
    Bellini Martini, 249
    Bisous du Soleil, 171
Champagne flute, Bisous du Soleil, 171
Champagne glass, Mr. Funk, 172
cherries/cherry juice

Blue Lagoon, 189
Cherry Bomb, 25
Citrus Sunset, 190
Drink the C, 152
Ocean Breeze, 55
Pink Panther, 205
Sea Breeze, 52
Sex On the Beach, 68
Sour Cherry Martini, 254
Cherry Bomb recipe, 25
Cherry Lime Spike recipe, 22
Cherry Swizzle recipe, 105
Cherry Tootsie Pop recipe, 106
cherry vodka
    Cherry Bomb, 25
    Cherry Lime Spike, 22
    Drink the C, 152
    Jolly Rancher, 114
    Sour Cherry Martini, 254
Chilton recipe, 197
Choco Peat recipe, 164
Chocolate Cream and Peaches recipe, 109
chocolate liqueur, Mocha Mocha Mocha, 220
chocolate vodka
    Angel's Kiss, 160
    Cherry Tootsie Pop, 106
    Chocolate Cream and Peaches, 109
    Storm Warning, 122
cinnamon
    Fancy White Russian, 219
    Liquid Apple Pie, 148
    Mason Jar Mudslide, 231
Citrus Sunset recipe, 190
Classic Cosmopolitan recipe, 17
Classic Vodka Martini recipe, 234
Classic White Russian recipe, 216
club soda
    Borrowed Thyme, 56
    Cherry Lime Spike, 22
    Early Riser, 80

Lemonade Shocker, 209
Ring #5, 144
Vineyard Splash, 198
Vodka Soda, 13
Coca-Cola
    Drink the C, 152
    Long Island Express, 10
Cock'n Bull pub, 37
cocktail glass
    Amelia, 175
    Appletini, 186
    Bellini Martini, 249
    Betty's Cosmo, 60
    Birthday Martini, 250
    Budget Cosmopolitan, 21
    Budget Vodka Martini, 237
    Choco Peat, 164
    Classic Cosmopolitan, 17
    Classic Vodka Martini, 234
    The Dirty Spy, 49
    Dirty Vodka Martini, 246
    Dry Vodka Martini, 241
    Early Riser, 80
    French Martini de Nancy, 257
    Grape Sourball, 193
    The Incredible Apicius Bloody Mary, 42
    Kamikaze, 182
    Lemon Drop, 210
    Lycheetini, 72
    McClure's Pickle Martini, 262
    Perfect Cosmopolitan, 18
    Perfect Vodka Martini, 245
    Pickled Martini, 265
    Purist's Vodka Martini, 238
    Quickslide, 98
    Raspberry Martini, 253
    Rose de Varsovie, 137
    Sour Cherry Martini, 254
    Spicy Martini, 261
    Summer Splash, 147

Vesper Martini, 258
Vodka Gimlet, 181
Wedded Bliss, 140
Wet Vodka Martini, 242
coconut rum, Drink the
C, 152
Coffee Concoctions
Classic White Russian,
216
Dangerous Grandma,
228
Deep Throat, 227
Espresso Martini, 224
Fancy White Russian,
219
Mason Jar Mudslide,
231
Mind Eraser, 223
Mocha Mocha Mocha,
220
White Russian, 215
coffee liqueur
Absolut Bitch, 126
Fancy White Russian,
219
Mason Jar Mudslide,
231
Mind Eraser, 223
Mocha Mocha Mocha,
220
Quickslide, 98
White Russian, 215
coffee vodka
Dangerous Grandma,
228
Deep Throat, 227
Cointreau
Betty's Cosmo, 60
Bisous du Soleil, 171
Drink the C, 152
Rose de Varsovie, 137
Collins glass
Harvey Wallbanger, 33
The Original Bloody
Mary, 45
Sex On the Beach, 68
copper mug
Mint Mule, 38
Moscow Mule, 37
coupe, Espresso Martini,
224
cranberries/cranberry
juice
Betty's Cosmo, 60
Bisous du Soleil, 171
Bona Dea, 167
Budget Cosmopolitan,
21

Cape Cod, 156
Capescrew, 34
Classic Cosmopolitan,
17
The Incredible Apicius
Bloody Mary, 42
Jolly Rancher, 114
Ocean Breeze, 55
Perfect Cosmopolitan,
18
Pink Lemonade, 206
Sea Breeze, 52
Sex On the Beach, 68
cranberry vodka
Summer Splash, 147
Woo Hoo, 125
cream
Birthday Martini, 250
Classic White Russian,
216
Creamsicle, 93
Deep Throat, 227
Mason Jar Mudslide,
231
White Russian, 215
cream liqueur, Quickslide,
98
cream soda, Butterbrew,
155
Creamsicle recipe, 93
crème de menthe, Vodka
Negroni, 14
Cynar, 100% Vitamin
Water, 84

Dangerous Grandma
recipe, 228
dark chocolate liqueur,
Choco Peat, 164
Deep Eddy Ruby Red
Grapefruit Vodka, Ruby
Twilite, 134
Deep Throat recipe, 227
DeKuyper Sour Apple
Pucker, Appletini, 186
The Dirty Spy recipe, 49
Dirty Vodka Martini
recipe, 246
Domaine de Canton,
Gingerbread, 159
double shot glass, Mind
Eraser, 223
Drink the C recipe, 152
dry vermouth
Budget Vodka Martini,
237
Classic Vodka Martini,
234
The Dirty Spy, 49

Dirty Vodka Martini,
246
Dry Vodka Martini, 241
Perfect Vodka Martini,
245
Pickled Martini, 265
Purist's Vodka Martini,
238
Spicy Martini, 261
Wet Vodka Martini, 242
Dry Vodka Martini recipe,
241

Early Riser recipe, 80
elderflower liqueur,
Sunny Day, 87
Espresso Martini recipe,
224
The Essential Bloody
Mary recipe, 41

Fancy White Russian
recipe, 219
French Martini de Nancy
recipe, 257
Fruity Refreshment
Absolut Bitch, 126
Betty's Cosmo, 60
Blastoff, 102
Borrowed Thyme, 56
Cherry Swizzle, 105
Cherry Tootsie Pop, 106
Chocolate Cream and
Peaches, 109
Early Riser, 80
Ginger Binger, 64
Godmother, 101
Grape Chill, 78
Gumball, 110
Hairy Navel, 75
Head Rush, 113
Herbal Affirmation, 88
By the Horns, 59
Jolly Rancher, 114
Lycheetini, 72
Melon Ball, 71
Melon Refresher, 76
Ocean Breeze, 55
100% Vitamin Water,
84
Peach Tree Iced Tea, 63
Pear Pressure, 97
Pink Petals, 117
Poison Apple, 118
Purple Hooter, 121
Quickslide, 98
Rose de Varsovie, 137
Rose Salt Dog, 133

Ruby Twilite, 134
Sage Advice, 67
Sea Breeze, 52
Sex On the Beach, 68
The Slammer, 83
Storm Warning, 122
Sunny Day, 87
Teddy Bear, 129
Vanilla Pear, 130
Woo Hoo, 125

Galliano, Harvey
Wallbanger, 33
Giffard Crème de
Pamplemousse Rose
French Martini de
Nancy, 257
Rose Salt Dog, 133
gin
Ocean Breeze, 55
Vesper Martini, 258
ginger beer
Mint Mule, 38
Moscow Mule, 37
Ginger Binger recipe, 64
Gingerbread recipe, 159
glass mug
Liquid Apple Pie, 148
glassware
bowl
100% Vitamin
Water, 84
carafe
100% Vitamin
Water, 84
Champagne flute
Bisous du Soleil,
171
Champagne glass
Mr. Funk, 172
cocktail glass
Amelia, 175
Appletini, 186
Bellini Martini, 249
Betty's Cosmo, 60
Birthday Martini,
250
Budget
Cosmopolitan, 21
Budget Vodka
Martini, 237
Choco Peat, 164
Classic
Cosmopolitan, 17
Classic Vodka
Martini, 234
The Dirty Spy, 49

Dirty Vodka Martini, 246
Dry Vodka Martini, 241
Early Riser, 80
French Martini de Nancy, 257
Grape Sourball, 193
The Incredible Apicius Bloody Mary, 42
Kamikaze, 182
Lemon Drop, 210
Lycheetini, 72
McClure's Pickle Martini, 262
Perfect Cosmopolitan, 18
Perfect Vodka Martini, 245
Pickled Martini, 265
Purist's Vodka Martini, 238
Quickslide, 98
Raspberry Martini, 253
Rose de Varsovie, 137
Sour Cherry Martini, 254
Spicy Martini, 261
Summer Splash, 147
Vesper Martini, 258
Vodka Gimlet, 181
Wedded Bliss, 140
Wet Vodka Martini, 242
Collins glass
Harvey Wallbanger, 33
Melon Ball, 71
The Original Bloody Mary, 45
Sex On the Beach, 68
copper mug
Mint Mule, 38
Moscow Mule, 37
coupe
Espresso Martini, 224
double shot glass
Mind Eraser, 223
glass mug
Liquid Apple Pie, 148
goblet
Melon Ball, 71

highball glass
Blue Fireflies, 178
Butterbrew, 155
Cape Cod, 156
Capescrew, 34
Cherry Lime Spike, 22
Chilton, 197
Ginger Binger, 64
Great Idea, 194
Greyhound, 26
Long Island Express, 10
Mint Mule, 38
Ocean Breeze, 55
Peach Tree Iced Tea, 63
Pink Panther, 205
Ring #4, 143
Ring #5, 144
Rose Salt Dog, 133
Sage Advice, 67
Screwdriver, 29
Sea Breeze, 52
Vodka Soda, 13
Vodka Sunrise, 151
mason jar
Blue Lagoon, 189
Citrus Sunset, 190
Hairy Navel, 75
Lemonade Shocker, 209
Liquid Apple Pie, 148
Mason Jar Bloody Mary, 46
Mason Jar Mudslide, 231
Mason Jar Screwdriver, 30
Melon Refresher, 76
Pink Lemonade, 206
Raspberry Twist, 202
Vineyard Splash, 198
overview of, 6
pint glass
Ruby Twilite, 134
pitcher
Jungle Punch, 168
punch bowl
Jungle Punch, 168
The Slammer, 83
rocks glass
Berries From the West, 201

Bona Dea, 167
Borrowed Thyme, 56
Classic White Russian, 216
Creamsicle, 93
Dangerous Grandma, 228
Drink the C, 152
The Essential Bloody Mary, 41
Fancy White Russian, 219
Godmother, 101
Grape Sourball, 193
Herbal Affirmation, 88
By the Horns, 59
A Little Lem, 185
Melon Ball, 71
Mocha Mocha Mocha, 220
Pear Pressure, 97
Strawberries and Cream, 94
Sunny Day, 87
Vodka Negroni, 14
White Russian, 215
shot glass
Absolut Bitch, 126
Angel's Kiss, 160
Blastoff, 102
Cherry Bomb, 25
Cherry Swizzle, 105
Cherry Tootsie Pop, 106
Chocolate Cream and Peaches, 109
Deep Throat, 227
Gingerbread, 159
Grape Chill, 78
Grape Sourball, 193
Gumball, 110
Head Rush, 113
Hell's Gate, 163
Jolly Rancher, 114
Kamikaze, 182
Pink Petals, 117
Poison Apple, 118
Purple Hooter, 121
Storm Warning, 122
Teddy Bear, 129
Vanilla Pear, 130
Woo Hoo, 125
Godmother recipe, 101
Grape Chill recipe, 78
Grape Sourball recipe, 193

grape vodka
Grape Chill, 78
Grape Sourball, 193
grapefruit/grapefruit juice
Blastoff, 102
Borrowed Thyme, 56
Citrus Sunset, 190
French Martini de Nancy, 257
Ginger Binger, 64
Greyhound, 26
Gumball, 110
By the Horns, 59
Ocean Breeze, 55
Pink Panther, 205
Rose Salt Dog, 133
Sea Breeze, 52
Wedded Bliss, 140
Great Idea recipe, 194
grenadine
Angel's Kiss, 160
Cherry Lime Spike, 22
Cherry Tootsie Pop, 106
Citrus Sunset, 190
Pink Petals, 117
Ring #4, 143
Ring #5, 144
Sage Advice, 67
Sour Cherry Martini, 254
Strawberries and Cream, 94
Vodka Sunrise, 151
Grey Goose Vodka
Perfect Cosmopolitan, 18
Pink Panther, 205
Greyhound recipe, 26
Gumball recipe, 110

Hairy Navel recipe, 75
Harry's New York Bar, 45
Harvey Wallbanger recipe, 33
Head Rush recipe, 113
Hell's Gate recipe, 163
Herbal Affirmation recipe, 88
Herring Cherry Liqueur, Rose de Varsovie, 137
highball glass
Blue Fireflies, 178
Butterbrew, 155
Cape Cod, 156
Capescrew, 34
Cherry Lime Spike, 22

Chilton, 197
Ginger Binger, 64
Great Idea, 194
Greyhound, 26
Long Island Express, 10
Mint Mule, 38
Ocean Breeze, 55
Peach Tree Iced Tea, 63
Pink Panther, 205
Ring #4, 143
Ring #5, 144
Rose Salt Dog, 133
Sage Advice, 67
Screwdriver, 29
Sea Breeze, 52
Vodka Soda, 13
Vodka Sunrise, 151

iced tea
  Peach Tree Iced Tea, 63
  Raspberry Twist, 202
The Incredible Apicius Bloody Mary recipe, 42
Irish cream
  Absolut Bitch, 126
  Mason Jar Mudslide, 231
  Storm Warning, 122

Jägermeister, Great Idea, 194
Jolly Rancher recipe, 114
Jungle Punch recipe, 168

Kahlúa
  Choco Peat, 164
  Classic White Russian, 216
  Espresso Martini, 224
Kamikaze recipe, 182
King Cole Bar, 45
kombucha
  Herbal Affirmation, 88
  Sage Advice, 67

Lemon Drop recipe, 210
lemonade
  Blue Lagoon, 189
  Grape Sourball, 193
  Raspberry Twist, 202
  Ring #4, 143
  Ruby Twilite, 134
  Summer Splash, 147
Lemonade Shocker recipe, 209

lemon-lime soda/Sprite
  Blue Fireflies, 178
  Jungle Punch, 168
  Melon Refresher, 76
  Ocean Breeze, 55
lemons/lemon juice
  Amelia, 175
  Berries From the West, 201
  Blackberry Puree, 175
  Blastoff, 102
  Blue Lagoon, 189
  Bona Dea, 167
  Budget Vodka Martini, 237
  Chilton, 197
  Citrus Sunset, 190
  Classic Vodka Martini, 234
  Dry Vodka Martini, 241
  The Essential Bloody Mary, 41
  French Martini de Nancy, 257
  Great Idea, 194
  Herbal Affirmation, 88
  Lemon Drop, 210
  Lemonade Shocker, 209
  A Little Lem, 185
  Long Island Express, 10
  Mr. Funk, 172
  The Original Bloody Mary, 45
  Perfect Vodka Martini, 245
  Pink Lemonade, 206
  Pink Panther, 205
  Raspberry Twist, 202
  Ring #4, 143
  Ruby Twilite, 134
  Vesper Martini, 258
  Vodka Sunrise, 151
Lillet Blanc, Vesper Martini, 258
limes/lime juice
  Betty's Cosmo, 60
  Bisous du Soleil, 171
  Blastoff, 102
  Blue Fireflies, 178
  Blue Lagoon, 189
  Budget Cosmopolitan, 21
  Cape Cod, 156
  Cherry Lime Spike, 22
  Cherry Swizzle, 105

Citrus Sunset, 190
Classic Cosmopolitan, 17
Ginger Binger, 64
By the Horns, 59
Kamikaze, 182
Mason Jar Bloody Mary, 46
Melon Refresher, 76
Mint Mule, 38
Moscow Mule, 37
Ocean Breeze, 55
100% Vitamin Water, 84
Pear Pressure, 97
Perfect Cosmopolitan, 18
Pink Panther, 205
Sea Breeze, 52
Sour Cherry Martini, 254
Summer Splash, 147
Sunny Day, 87
Vineyard Splash, 198
Vodka Gimlet, 181
Vodka Soda, 13
Wet Vodka Martini, 242
Liquid Apple Pie recipe, 148
A Little Lem recipe, 185
Long Island Express recipe, 10
Luxardo, Rose Salt Dog, 133
lychee liqueur, Lycheetini, 72
lychees
  Lycheetini, 72
  Wedded Bliss, 140
Lycheetini recipe, 72

Magnificent Martinis
  Bellini Martini, 249
  Birthday Martini, 250
  Budget Vodka Martini, 237
  Classic Vodka Martini, 234
  Dirty Vodka Martini, 246
  Dry Vodka Martini, 241
  French Martini de Nancy, 257
  McClure's Pickle Martini, 262
  Perfect Vodka Martini, 245
  Pickled Martini, 265

Purist's Vodka Martini, 238
Raspberry Martini, 253
Sour Cherry Martini, 254
Spicy Martini, 261
Vesper Martini, 258
Wet Vodka Martini, 242
maraschino cherries. See also cherries/cherry juice
  Blue Lagoon, 189
  Cherry Bomb, 25
  Drink the C, 152
  Sour Cherry Martini, 254
Martin, John, 37
mason jar
  Blue Lagoon, 189
  Citrus Sunset, 190
  Hairy Navel, 75
  Lemonade Shocker, 209
  Liquid Apple Pie, 148
  Mason Jar Bloody Mary, 46
  Mason Jar Mudslide, 231
  Mason Jar Screwdriver, 30
  Melon Refresher, 76
  Pink Lemonade, 206
  Raspberry Twist, 202
  Vineyard Splash, 198
  Vodka Soda, 13
Mason Jar Bloody Mary recipe, 46
Mason Jar Mudslide recipe, 231
Mason Jar Screwdriver recipe, 30
McClure's Pickle Martini recipe, 262
Melon Ball recipe, 71
melon liqueur, Melon Refresher, 76
Melon Refresher recipe, 76
Merman, Ethel, 216
Mesta, Perle, 216
Midori, Melon Ball, 71
milk
  Angel's Kiss, 160
  Chocolate Cream and Peaches, 109
  Fancy White Russian, 219
  Mocha Mocha Mocha, 220

Mind Eraser recipe, 223
mint
    Amelia, 175
    Ginger Binger, 64
    Hairy Navel, 75
    A Little Lem, 185
    Mint Mule, 38
    Moscow Mule, 37
    Peach Tree Iced Tea, 63
    Rose Salt Dog, 133
Mint Mule recipe, 38
Mocha Mocha Mocha
recipe, 220
Morgan, Jack, 37
Moscow Mule recipe, 37
Mr. Funk recipe, 172

Ocean Breeze recipe, 55
olives/olive brine
    Budget Vodka Martini,
    237
    The Dirty Spy, 49
    Dirty Vodka Martini,
    246
    Mason Jar Bloody
    Mary, 46
    Purist's Vodka Martini,
    238
    Spicy Martini, 261
100% Vitamin Water
recipe, 84
oranges/orange juice
    Bisous du Soleil, 171
    Blastoff, 102
    Blue Fireflies, 178
    Capescrew, 34
    Creamsicle, 93
    Dangerous Grandma,
    228
    Early Riser, 80
    Grape Sourball, 193
    Hairy Navel, 75
    Harvey Wallbanger, 33
    Mason Jar Screwdriver,
    30
    Melon Ball, 71
    Sage Advice, 67
    Screwdriver, 29
    Sex On the Beach, 68
    The Slammer, 83
    Sunny Day, 87
    Vodka Negroni, 14
    Vodka Sunrise, 151
The Original Bloody Mary
recipe, 45

Party Favors
    Amelia, 175
    Angel's Kiss, 160
    Bisous du Soleil, 171
    Bona Dea, 167
    Butterbrew, 155
    Cape Cod, 156
    Choco Peat, 164
    Drink the C, 152
    Gingerbread, 159
    Hell's Gate, 163
    Jungle Punch, 168
    Liquid Apple Pie, 148
    Mr. Funk, 172
    Ring #4, 143
    Ring #5, 144
    Summer Splash, 147
    Vodka Sunrise, 151
    Wedded Bliss, 140
peach schnapps
    Bellini Martini, 249
    Hairy Navel, 75
    Peach Tree Iced Tea, 63
    Sex On the Beach, 68
    Woo Hoo, 125
Peach Tree Iced Tea
recipe, 63
peach vodka
    Bona Dea, 167
    Chocolate Cream and
    Peaches, 109
    Head Rush, 113
    Jolly Rancher, 114
    Mr. Funk, 172
Pear Pressure recipe, 97
pear vodka, Head Rush,
113
pears/pear juice
    Pear Pressure, 97
    Vanilla Pear, 130
The Peat Monster whisky,
Choco Peat, 164
Perfect Cosmopolitan
recipe, 18
Perfect Vodka Martini
recipe, 245
Petlot, Fernand, 45
Pickled Martini recipe,
265
pickles/pickle juice
    McClure's Pickle
    Martini, 262
Pickled Martini, 265
pineapple/pineapple
juice
    Grape Chill, 78
    Hairy Navel, 75

Pink Lemonade recipe,
206
Pink Panther recipe, 205
Pink Petals recipe, 117
pint glass, Ruby Twilite,
134
pitcher, Jungle Punch, 168
Poison Apple recipe, 118
punch bowl
    Jungle Punch, 168
    The Slammer, 83
Purist's Vodka Martini
recipe, 238
Purple Hooter recipe, 121
purple-grape-and-
watermelon puree,
Vineyard Splash, 198

Quickslide recipe, 98

raspberries
    Pink Panther, 205
    Purple Hooter, 121
    Raspberry Martini, 253
    Raspberry Twist, 202
    Ring #5, 144
Raspberry Martini recipe,
253
Raspberry Twist recipe,
202
raspberry vodka
    Gumball, 110
    Purple Hooter, 121
    Raspberry Martini, 253
    Raspberry Twist, 202
    Ring #4, 143
    Ring #5, 144
Red Bull
    Cherry Bomb, 25
    Cherry Tootsie Pop, 106
    By the Horns, 59
Red Snapper, 45
Ring #4 recipe, 143
Ring #5 recipe, 144
rocks glass
    Berries From the West,
    201
    Bona Dea, 167
    Borrowed Thyme, 56
    Classic White Russian,
    216
    Creamsicle, 93
    Dangerous Grandma,
    228
    Drink the C, 152
    The Essential Bloody
    Mary, 41

Fancy White Russian,
219
Godmother, 101
Grape Sourball, 193
Herbal Affirmation, 88
By the Horns, 59
A Little Lem, 185
Mocha Mocha Mocha,
220
Pear Pressure, 97
Strawberries and
Cream, 94
Sunny Day, 87
Vodka Negroni, 14
White Russian, 215
root beer vodka, Teddy
Bear, 129
Rose de Varsovie recipe,
137
Rose Salt Dog recipe, 133
Rose's Sweetened Lime
Juice, Betty's Cosmo, 60
Ruby Twilite recipe, 134
RumChata, Gingerbread,
159

Sage Advice recipe, 67
salt
    Chilton, 197
    The Original Bloody
    Mary, 45
    Rose Salt Dog, 133
sambuca, Head Rush, 113
Screwdriver recipe, 29
Sea Breeze recipe, 52
7UP Zero Sugar
    Cherry Swizzle, 105
    Purple Hooter, 121
Sex On the Beach recipe,
68
Shiner Ruby Redbird beer,
Ruby Twilite, 134
shot glass
    Absolut Bitch, 126
    Angel's Kiss, 160
    Blastoff, 102
    Cherry Bomb, 25
    Cherry Swizzle, 105
    Cherry Tootsie Pop, 106
    Chocolate Cream and
    Peaches, 109
    Deep Throat, 227
    Gingerbread, 159
    Grape Chill, 78
    Grape Sourball, 193
    Gumball, 110
    Head Rush, 113

Hell's Gate, 163
Jolly Rancher, 114
Kamikaze, 182
Pink Petals, 117
Poison Apple, 118
Purple Hooter, 121
Storm Warning, 122
Teddy Bear, 129
Vanilla Pear, 130
Woo Hoo, 125
Simple Syrup
Bellini Martini, 249
Berries From the West, 201
Raspberry Martini, 253
Simple Syrup recipe, 7
Skinnygirl Bare Naked vodka, Purple Hooter, 121
Skinnygirl Cucumber vodka, Hell's Gate, 163
Skinnygirl Island Coconut vodka, Pink Petals, 117
Skinnygirl White Cherry vodka
Cherry Swizzle, 105
Pink Petals, 117
Poison Apple, 118
Storm Warning, 122
Skyy Vodka
Betty's Cosmo, 60
Classic Cosmopolitan, 17
Classic Vodka Martini, 234
The Slammer recipe, 83
Sour Cherry Martini recipe, 254
Southern Comfort, The Slammer, 83
Sparkling French Berry Lemonade, Pink Panther, 205
sparkling wine
Bona Dea, 167
Mr. Funk, 172
Spicy Martini recipe, 261
Sprite/lemon-lime soda
Blue Fireflies, 178
Jungle Punch, 168
Melon Refresher, 76
Ocean Breeze, 55
St-Germain
Amelia, 175
Pink Panther, 205
Stolichnaya Stoli Hot vodka, Choco Peat, 164
Storm Warning recipe, 122

Strawberries and Cream recipe, 94
strawberries/strawberry juice
Sage Advice, 67
Strawberries and Cream, 94
strawberry seltzer, Sage Advice, 67
strawberry vodka, Strawberries and Cream, 94
strawberry/sage kombucha, Sage Advice, 67
sugar
Lemon Drop, 210
Vineyard Splash, 198
Summer Splash recipe, 147
Sunny Day recipe, 87
Svedka Vodka
Budget Cosmopolitan, 21
Budget Vodka Martini, 237
Sweet and Sours
Appletini, 186
Berries From the West, 201
Blue Fireflies, 178
Blue Lagoon, 189
Chilton, 197
Citrus Sunset, 190
Grape Sourball, 193
Great Idea, 194
Kamikaze, 182
Lemon Drop, 210
Lemonade Shocker, 209
A Little Lem, 185
Pink Lemonade, 206
Pink Panther, 205
Raspberry Twist, 202
Vineyard Splash, 198
Vodka Gimlet, 181
sweet vermouth
Early Riser, 80
Perfect Vodka Martini, 245
Sunny Day, 87
Vodka Negroni, 14

Tabasco/Tabasco Chipotle
Hell's Gate, 163
The Incredible Apicius Bloody Mary, 42
Teddy Bear recipe, 129

tomatoes/tomato juice
The Essential Bloody Mary, 41
The Incredible Apicius Bloody Mary, 42
Mason Jar Bloody Mary, 46
The Original Bloody Mary, 45
Topo Chico, Chilton, 197
Tops, Gustave, 216
Tried and True
Budget Cosmopolitan, 21
Capescrew, 34
Cherry Bomb, 25
Cherry Lime Spike, 22
Classic Cosmopolitan, 17
The Dirty Spy, 49
The Essential Bloody Mary, 41
Greyhound, 26
Harvey Wallbanger, 33
The Incredible Apicius Bloody Mary, 42
Long Island Express, 10
Mason Jar Bloody Mary, 46
Mason Jar Screwdriver, 30
Mint Mule, 38
Moscow Mule, 37
The Original Bloody Mary, 45
Perfect Cosmopolitan, 18
Screwdriver, 29
Vodka Negroni, 14
Vodka Soda, 13
triple sec
Appletini, 186
Budget Cosmopolitan, 21
Capescrew, 34
Classic Cosmopolitan, 17
Creamsicle, 93
Ginger Binger, 64
Kamikaze, 182
Lemon Drop, 210
Long Island Express, 10
Lycheetini, 72
Perfect Cosmopolitan, 18
Raspberry Martini, 253

Ring #4, 143
Truman, Harry S., 216
Tuaca, Absolut Bitch, 126

Vanilla Pear recipe, 130
vanilla vodka
Birthday Martini, 250
Butterbrew, 155
Gingerbread, 159
Liquid Apple Pie, 148
Pear Pressure, 97
Strawberries and Cream, 94
Teddy Bear, 129
Vanilla Pear, 130
Vesper Martini recipe, 258
Vineyard Splash recipe, 198
vodka, overview of, 6–7
Vodka Gimlet recipe, 181
Vodka Negroni recipe, 14
Vodka Soda recipe, 13
Vodka Sunrise recipe, 151

Wedded Bliss recipe, 140
Western Son Blueberry Flavored Vodka, Berries From the West, 201
Wet Vodka Martini recipe, 242
whipped cream vodka, Deep Throat, 227
whiskey, Dangerous Grandma, 228
white balsamic reduction, The Incredible Apicius Bloody Mary, 42
white chocolate liqueur, Birthday Martini, 250
White Russian recipe, 215
Woo Hoo recipe, 125
Worcestershire sauce
The Essential Bloody Mary, 41
Mason Jar Bloody Mary, 46
The Original Bloody Mary, 45

ABOUT
CIDER MILL PRESS
BOOK PUBLISHERS

Good ideas ripen with time. From seed to harvest, Cider Mill Press brings fine reading, information, and entertainment together between the covers of its creatively crafted books. Our Cider Mill bears fruit twice a year, publishing a new crop of titles each spring and fall.

"Where Good Books Are Ready for Press"
501 Nelson Place
Nashville, Tennessee 37214
cidermillpress.com